W9-BEI-900

FERGUSON
CAREER BIOGRAPHIES

TOM
HANKS

Actor

James Robert Parish

Ferguson
An imprint of ☑®Facts On File

Tom Hanks: Actor

Copyright © 2004 by Facts On File, Inc.

Ferguson
An imprint of Facts On File, Inc.
132 West 31st Street
New York NY 10001

Parish, James Robert.
  Tom Hanks, actor/James Robert Parish.
     p. cm.
Includes index.
Contents: Sent down from a higher league—The king of Wally' Coliseum—The majors—A unique combination—The Stanley Cup—California, here we come—Last days in the Big Apple—Time line—How to become an athlete—To learn more about athletes.
  ISBN 0-8160-5542-4 (HC: alk. paper)
  1. Hanks, Tom—Juvenile literature. 2. Actors—United States—Biography—Juvenile literature. [1. Hanks, Tom. 2. Actors and actresses.] I. Title.
  PN2287.H18P37 2004
  791.4302'8'082—dc22   2003023120

Ferguson books are available at special discounts when purchased in bulk quantities for businesses, associations, institutions, or sales promotions. Please call our Special Sales Department in New York at (212) 967-8800 or (800) 322-8755.

You can find Ferguson on the World Wide Web at http://www.fergpubco.com

Text design by David Strelecky

Pages 89–117 adapted from *Ferguson's Encyclopedia of Careers and Vocation Guidance, Twelfth Edition*

Printed in the United States of America

MP FOF 10 9 8 7 6 5 4 3 2 1

This book is printed on acid-free paper.

CONTENTS

HOLLYWOOD'S FAMOUS EVERYMAN

For his impressive screen performances in *Philadelphia* (1993) and *Forrest Gump* (1994)—two very different films—Tom Hanks won consecutive Best Actor Academy Awards. This had not happened in Hollywood since the 1930s, when actor Spencer Tracy achieved the same distinction. In the decade since these noteworthy victories Tom has maintained his lofty entertainment-industry status. The veteran actor, who currently earns $20 million per feature film, is one of Hollywood's most powerful people.

Tom Hanks is prized as Hollywood's everyman, meaning that he is skilled at playing ordinary characters to whom almost everyone can relate—and he does so in a powerful fashion. Since Tom first rose to show business

Tom Hanks accepts an Emmy Award as part of a team of directors of the miniseries Band of Brothers. (Landov)

prominence in the mid-1980s, many film critics have compared him favorably to two big stars of Hollywood's Golden Age: Jimmy Stewart and Cary Grant. Like the lanky Stewart, Tom is adept at portraying the man next door, the type of likable individual you trust right away and want to get to know as a friend. And, like the sophisticated Grant, on screen Hanks can be witty, glib, and charming. In discussing the top movie performers of the last 15 years, *Premiere* magazine observed, "You begin to get an idea of Tom Hanks's singular and irreplaceable role in the history of popular movies when you imagine subtracting him from that history."

In April 1999 Steven Spielberg presented Tom Hanks with the prestigious Lifetime Achievement award given by the American Museum of the Moving Image. The esteemed filmmaker said of his actor friend and frequent coworker, "Tom is from that old-time America, when tradition and pride in your country were things you didn't scoff at." On another occasion Steve Tisch, one of the *Forrest Gump* producers, observed of Tom: "The man is as nice, as honest, as professional, as personal, as he seems to be."

Not Just "Mr. Nice Guy"

Although the unassuming Hanks is persistently labeled "Mr. Nice Guy," he is not fond of the title. Says Hanks, "I'm probably as nice as the next guy, but you know, I have my moments. It can be a pain with people having that expectation." Sally Field, who costarred with Hanks in *Punchline* (1988) and *Forrest Gump*, agrees that there are more dimensions to Tom than his pleasant image presumes. "Yes, he's very entertaining and funny and easy to be around. But you know there's somebody else underneath, somebody dark," says Field. "There's a sad side, a dark side. And that's what makes him so compelling on the screen."

Much of this "dark" side stems from Tom's unusual childhood, a complicated time when his parents divorced and remarried other partners frequently. Within a five-year period, young Tom gained two different stepmothers and several stepsiblings and changed addresses and schools repeatedly. This meant he was constantly the new kid on the block. Traumatic as that may sound, Tom, an extremely private person who avoids open discussions of personal problems, publicly shrugs off his difficult childhood. "We were just a completely more or less normal broken family. Everybody was married a bunch and everybody lived different places, and nobody thought much of it," he says.

As a youngster Hanks never dreamed of becoming an actor. His great passions were sports and, especially, the U.S. space program. He hoped one day to become an astronaut. (Tom was able to live out this fantasy when he starred as astronaut Jim Lovell in the 1995 movie *Apollo 13*.) During high school Tom became intrigued with the theater world and make-believe. Once he came under the spell of the acting profession, it became the only career option for this highly imaginative teenager with the self-deprecating—and goofy—sense of humor. Years later, long after he had mastered his creative craft, Tom would still remain boyishly enthusiastic about his choice of professions. "I have this insane job that lets me put on other people's clothes and pretend to be somebody else for a time, and they pay me ludicrous amounts of money to do it."

2

ALWAYS ON THE MOVE

Thomas Jeffrey Hanks, a very distant relative of President Abraham Lincoln, was born July 9, 1956, in Concord, a town in northern California about 23 miles northeast of San Francisco. Tom was third of the four children of Amos and Janet Hanks. His mom was a waitress. His dad (known to friends as "Bud") was a restaurant cook who once aspired to be a writer and had always dreamed of moving to Australia. Those hopes vanished when Amos married Janet and the two soon became parents. Once caught in the responsibilities of a sizable household, Amos Hanks and his family moved frequently as he changed jobs within the food industry. Meanwhile Janet stayed at home to care for their children.

In 1961 Amos and Janet, already married for 10 years, became parents for the fourth time with the arrival of their son James. By then the emotional and financial pressures of domestic life had badly damaged the couple's relationship. One day in January 1962 Amos disappeared without informing his children where he was going. When he finally returned home a month later, he had been to Reno, Nevada, where he filed for divorce from Janet. That night, without explanation, he told his three oldest kids (Sandra, Lawrence, and Tom) to gather a few of their belongings—at most there was room for each to bring along only one or two favorite toys—and to hurry out to the pickup truck in the driveway. (Jimmy, still an infant, remained behind permanently with Janet Hanks.) Amos drove his three children to Reno, where he had already found a new job as a hotel/casino chef and had rented a small basement apartment. Amos enrolled Tom in the Holy Child Day Care Center in Reno because, unlike the older children, Tom was too young to be on his own while Amos was working.

There were soon new changes in the fragmented Hanks household. On April 23, 1962, four days after Amos's divorce from Janet became final, he married his landlady, Winifred Finley, who was recently divorced and had five children of her own. Suddenly Tom and his siblings had a whole new family. However, their dad, who was never good at communication, did not explain this latest change. Overnight Tom and the seven other children were sharing the cramped basement quarters of a small house, while the newlyweds lived upstairs. Years later Hanks said of the disorienting setup, "I remember in school we had to draw a picture of our house and family and I ran out of places to put people. I put them on the roof. I drew dad in bed, sleeping, since he worked so hard in the restaurant."

After a time the family moved to a larger house in Sacramento, California, then to one in Pleasant Hills, California. Of Amos's three children, Tom best adjusted to the ever-changing domestic situation. As the new Mrs. Hanks observed of the five-year-old boy, he "could roll with the punches." Tom had his own take on being the youngest member of his overcrowded household, saying in later years, "You could get lost in the shuffle or you could be a loudmouth. I chose the latter route."

Within two-and-a-half years Amos and Winifred divorced. Once again, without providing any real explanation, Amos had his trio of children pack their belongings, and they drove off into the night, this time to Oakland, across the bay from San Francisco. This move was especially disruptive for the now more mature and aware Tom. His defense mechanism was to put his second family in the past. In 1984 Hanks told *Us* magazine, "I wouldn't remember their names if they showed their faces today."

For a time the Hanks family stayed in San Mateo, California, with Amos's sister Mary, who was a devout member of the strict religious group called the Nazarenes.

After their unstructured childhood the bewildered children had a tough time following the rules and order in their aunt's household. Said Tom: "We weren't allowed to watch the *Three Stooges*; there were an awful lot of rules . . . awfully long prayers." On occasional weekends and usually for all the major holidays Tom and his siblings would be sent by bus to their mother, who lived in Red Bluff, in upstate California. Because these visits were infrequent, Tom rarely saw his younger brother Jimmy, who lived with their mother. Thus, the two boys were virtual strangers to one another. They didn't become friendly until the late 1980s. By that time Jimmy had followed in Tom's footsteps, also becoming an actor.

After a few months the Hanks moved out of Mary's home, relocating to a series of small, low-rent apartments, many of them in Oakland. Since Amos Hanks spent long hours at his restaurant jobs, the three youngsters were left pretty much to their own devices. This undisciplined routine was fine for Tom, who enjoyed the companionship of his brother and sister. He would later insist that this lonely upbringing had little ill effect on his psyche: "The coolest place to be was at home, because we were always cracking each other up. I was surrounded by goodness."

Discussing the offbeat nature of his childhood, Tom noted, "We did our own laundry. We supposedly had to keep the house clean, though it never was. . . . We were completely unsupervised, but we got into surprisingly little trouble." Tom loved spending hours in front of the TV, losing himself in shows such as *Star Trek* and news coverage of America's missions into outer space. Another favorite activity for the Hanks household were those evenings when Amos would toss a mattress on the back of his truck and drive the family to a local drive-in theater where, reclining in the truck bed, the father and children watched movies.

As the youngest of the three children living with Amos, less was expected of Tom around the house. He says, "Because I had less at stake, I developed an observational point of view." This behavioral attitude carried into adulthood, where Tom feels more comfortable in social situations being the onlooker.

A Sudden Change

In 1966 Amos Hanks was studying to teach food and hotel management at a local vocational college. He recently had met Frances Wong, a waitress and a divorced mother of three girls. The two soon fell in love and married. While her two older daughters went to live with their father, Frances's youngest child became part of the new household. Contrary to Amos's expectations, his own children were quickly disillusioned by the latest change in their lives. Frances was very organized and tried to convert her stepchildren to her extremely disciplined ways. It created domestic chaos. A frustrated Sandra soon moved out, choosing to stay with her mother. Tom and his older brother Larry set up headquarters in the basement of their new home, only mingling with the others at mealtimes. Later Larry moved to Red Bluff to be with his mother and sister.

By age 10 Tom had had a mother, two stepmothers, and had resided in 10 different houses in five different cities. One result of all these moves was that he had learned how to adapt to new schools and classmates quickly. Although he was quite shy by nature, he developed the outward personality of a class clown. However, Tom was wise enough to never overstep the bounds with his instructors: "If the teacher wasn't laughing, I'd shut up," he has said.

A few years later Tom attended Bret Harte Junior High in Oakland. By this time he had acquired the flexibility to mingle with a variety of social groups at school. However, beneath his mask as a jokester, he felt insecure. He considered himself an outsider who had been left alone far too often. As an adolescent, he still devoted a great deal of his free time to watching TV, especially anything to do with outer space. When Stanley Kubrick's movie _2001: A Space Odyssey_ was released in 1968, Tom was so excited that he saw the feature 22 times at local theaters.

At age 14 Hanks joined the First Covenant Church, a Fundamentalist Christian group in Oakland. It gave him a sense of belonging and acceptance that he badly needed. He particularly thrived on the social aspects of the group, but after a few years he drifted away from the organization, reasoning, "When you're young and idealistic, you tend to view things in absolute terms, and the absolutes didn't pan out, even within the confines of that place."

As a boy, Tom was fascinated with space travel. This interest led to his role in the film Apollo 13 *many years later.* (Photofest)

Opening New Vistas

At Oakland's Skyline High School Hanks remained an average student academically. Still thriving as a class clown with a sharp sense of comedic timing, he participated in a few sports activities, including soccer and track. (Now approaching his full height of 6 feet, 1 inch, his track teammates called him "Lanky Hanks.") For a while, when school was not in session, he was employed as a soda vendor at the Oakland A's baseball games. Although he had a girlfriend during his high school years, the future actor later acknowledged that he was not popular with the opposite sex: "I was a little too geeky, a little too gangly, and much too manic."

Inspired by a friend's performance in a high school play, Tom decided to give theater a try. He enrolled in Rawley Farnsworth's drama class at Skyline High, eventually taking six courses with his new mentor. Under Farnsworth's guidance, Hanks worked as stage manager for a school production of the musical _My Fair Lady_. Later, for the school's presentation of Tennessee Williams's _Night of the Iguana_, Tom had a small role as the bus driver.

Farnsworth was one of the first to note that Hanks had a special charisma onstage, that he was one of those individuals "you can't take your eyes off and you want to see everything they do." Next the teacher cast Tom in the comedic part of Sir Andrew Aguecheck in Shakespeare's _Twelfth Night_. Under Farnsworth's supervision, Hanks learned that to become a good performer, a newcomer must try a variety of roles. Then, no matter how successful he might become, he should always reach for fresh acting challenges. These were valuable lessons that Tom kept in mind, especially once his screen-acting career began to flourish in the 1980s.

In his senior year at Skyline Hanks had a pivotal role in the Rodgers and Hammerstein musical _South Pacific_. For

Tom's rousing performance as Luther Billis, he received the school's equivalent of an Academy Award. In years to come Hanks would always credit Farnsworth, as well as fellow classmate John Gilkerson, for being very supportive of his early acting ambitions. In fact, when Hanks accepted his Oscar for his role in *Philadelphia* in 1994, he credited these two men as inspirations for his award-winning performance in that film.

In these early days of his acting career Tom tried to create a stage persona for himself. For example, on play programs in his senior year Hanks spelled his first name "Thom." He soon decided this name change was pretentious and returned to the normal spelling.

By Tom's last year at Skyline he was living away from his family, boarding with a single mother (whom he knew from his church group) and her three children. To earn spending money Hanks worked weekends and during the summer as a bellman at the Oakland Hilton Hotel. The job was a lot of fun for Tom, especially when he had opportunities to drive screen legend Sidney Poitier to the airport in the hotel limousine, or carry luggage for the likes of singing star Cher or tennis champ Billy Jean King. Some of these often-amusing celebrity encounters would crop up as anecdotes when Hanks began achieving fame as a screen actor in the 1980s and was making the rounds of the late-night TV talk shows.

On to College

Because Tom achieved only a C average throughout high school, his options for college admission were limited. Of the three schools to which he applied, he was only accepted at Chabot Community College, located in nearby Hayward. Tom was still unaware of what career path he wanted to take. He claimed he was "waiting for something to conk me on the head and say, 'This is the direction you want to go in.'" By now Tom was again living at home with his dad and stepmother.

At Chabot Tom initially did not participate in campus stage productions, but he frequently visited San Francisco or Berkeley to see plays performed. One day he encountered his high school friend John Gilkerson, also at Chabot, who convinced Tom to return to the stage. This nudge prompted Hanks to audition for a school production of Thornton Wilder's _Our Town_, in which he won a leading role and received enthusiastic reviews.

A turning point for Tom was enrolling in a Chabot course named Drama in Performance, which was taught by Herb Kennedy. The course required students to read several plays and then to see a local production of each. One of Hanks's most career-shaping experiences was reading Eugene O'Neill's _The Iceman Cometh_ and then watching it performed live at the Berkeley Repertory

Theater. Tom later recalled, "I came out of the theater enthralled with what those people had done that night. . . . I had never seen that anywhere else." Tom shared this amazing experience with his teacher, and Kennedy guided the student into further theatrical discoveries. Tom didn't forget Kennedy's guidance once he achieved success. Years later, in the summer of 1981, when Tom costarred in the TV sitcom *Bosom Buddies*, Kennedy coaxed him back to Chabot to star in a campus production of the play *Charley's Aunt*.

Much of Tom's time at Chabot was spent in theater craft courses and working backstage for campus productions. He found great satisfaction in his carpentry skills and his ability to take whatever materials he found at hand and convert them into use for stage projects.

In 1976 Tom earned a scholarship in theater craft, which allowed him to transfer to California State University at Sacramento. The school had a small theater department, but one that allowed for great student participation. Initially Hanks planned to work backstage as stage manager, lighting designer, or set builder. He knew he liked being around the theater. It gave him a great sense of belonging. Another of Tom's characteristics was his irrepressible clown instinct. He was always making humorous remarks or doing goofy stunts, no matter what the situation.

A Breakthrough

One of Hanks's theater arts classmates was Susan Dillingham, who adopted the professional name Samantha Lewes. The two became inseparable. A romantic relationship quickly developed and turned into love. Meanwhile Tom's enthusiasm for performing in front of, rather than behind, the stage reasserted itself. (As Hanks phrased it, "I soon discovered the most magical place to be was on the stage.") When several of his pals were cast in a campus production but he was not, Hanks took matters into hand. He auditioned for an upcoming production of Anton Chekhov's *The Cherry Orchard* that was to be presented at the Sacramento Civic Theater. He was happily surprised to win the role of the servant Yasha, for which he received favorable reviews.

Vincent Dowling, the out-of-town director who guided *The Cherry Orchard*, was impressed by Tom's budding talents. At the time Dowling was artistic director of the Great Lakes Shakespeare Festival in Cleveland. He offered Tom and a few others the opportunity to become summer interns there. Hanks, Lewes, and other campus friends happily made the trek east when the school year ended.

As backstage workers painting sets, hanging lights, and so on, the interns were not paid. But if they also had stage roles, they received small salaries. This prompted Hanks to audition for small parts that soon began to come his way.

For Tom, just getting paid for acting "was a phenomenon to me. This was huge in my eyes." Whenever he was not in a play and had time off, Hanks found great pleasure in attending Cleveland Indians baseball games, even though the professional team was doing poorly. He became so loyal to the downtrodden local ballplayers that, years later, interviewers would interpret this devoted support as more evidence of Hanks's everyman quality. In regard to the team, Hanks said he was "perfectly happy with their position at the bottom of the [American League] standing."

That fall, when Tom and Samantha returned to Sacramento, he chose not to return to college. Samantha was pregnant, and he needed to provide for his girlfriend and their baby. He went to work at the local Civic Theater as assistant stage manager for an $800 monthly salary. On November 24, 1977, the couple's son Colin was born.

In the summer of 1978 Tom and Samantha, along

Tom and fellow actor Lora Staley in costume for Two Gentlemen of Verona, *1978.* (Photofest)

with their baby, arrived in Ohio for another season at the Shakespeare Festival. By now Hanks was winning larger acting assignments with the troupe, whose shows often toured the area. He appeared as Proteus in _Two Gentlemen of Verona_ and Grumio in _The Taming of the Shrew_. For his showy performances that season Hanks received the Best Actor of the Year award from the Cleveland Critics Circle.

When the 1978 season at the Great Lakes Shakespeare Festival concluded, Tom and Samantha made a major decision. They needed to expand their professional horizons beyond Cleveland and Sacramento. Rather than try their luck in Los Angeles, the movie capital, where they feared they would be lost, they chose to live in New York City. There, friends advised Hanks, he at least could get work with the Riverside Shakespeare Company while waiting for his Broadway break. Since Hanks and Lewes were down to their last $35, they sold his well-traveled Volkswagen Beetle to finance the risky relocation. The couple used the $850 from the sale of the car to start life in the Big Apple, where they hoped to find fame and fortune.

3

BUILDING A REPUTATION AND CAREER

In the fall of 1978 Tom and Samantha and their infant son Colin settled into a walkup apartment on West 45th Street, which was part of a rundown Manhattan neighborhood long known as Hell's Kitchen. Initially, the only pieces of furniture in their cockroach-ridden apartment were a few milk crates. With scant savings remaining after the move from Cleveland, the family survived on the weekly unemployment checks Tom received after his recent work at the Great Lakes Shakespeare Festival. There were times when the family was so low on funds that they gratefully accepted a few dollars from Tom's sister Sandra, who scraped together cash by collecting and redeeming empty soda bottles.

Hanks found acting jobs at the Riverside Shakespeare Company, including a role in the troupe's staging of Machiavelli's *Mandrake*. It was good experience, but Tom received little or no salary for his efforts. Like most new actors, he auditioned for TV commercials and daytime soap operas. However, he met with no success on these tryouts.

Adjusting to life in New York was not easy for Tom and Samantha. In addition to the strain of competing for possible work assignments in the show business world, they had to care for their baby. Meanwhile Tom underwent a crash course in putting together a resume, having head shots taken by a photographer, preparing audition scenes, and so forth, so that he could make casting rounds.

The daily struggle in New York quickly matured Hanks. "I had an ongoing responsibility that a lot of actors can shirk," said Tom. "We lived on the edge, but thank God no one got sick." At the same time Tom angled to get a break in his chosen profession. The actor has not forgotten those painful times. "Sometimes I'd take a hundred dollars and drive from city to city looking for work. I went for the jobs that nobody else wanted. Sometimes I'd wake up at night, go into the bathroom, look at myself in the mirror and think, 'What's happened to me? My career's over before it's begun.'"

Returning to an Old Haunt

With no paying work materializing in Manhattan, a discouraged Tom and family went back to the Great Lakes Shakespeare Festival for the summer 1979 season. During this stay he performed in such productions as *A Midsummer Night's Dream* and a show titled *Do Me a Favorite*. In the latter show, dealing with Shakespearean actors touring around greater Dublin, his part called for him to perform as a boy playing a girl who, in turn, is portraying a boy. Festival director Vincent Dowling said his protégée was "the best Shakespearean clown I ever knew, because he was seriously real and seriously funny at the same time."

When Hanks returned to Manhattan that fall, he was pleasantly surprised to win a feature-film assignment. The job was brought about by Simon Maslow, who had recently become Tom's personal manager. Maslow had found talent representation for the young actor with the J. Michael Bloom firm, which had offices in both New York and Los Angeles. The Bloom Agency had Tom cast in the motion picture *He Knows You're Alone* (1980). It was a low-budget slasher film that was to be shot entirely on Staten Island. For an experienced Shakespearean actor the assignment might have seemed a professional step down. However, Tom was excited at the opportunity of making his movie debut and being paid $800 for his small role. As he joked later, "It was the first job I had wearing regular pants, you know, as opposed to [medieval] sword belts, leather jerkins [a close-fitting, sleeveless coat], and sandals."

The horror picture concerns a knife-wielding murderer who butchers several women in a bridal party. Hanks plays Elliott, a psychology student, who attempts to explain to a cast member (and the audience) what motivates the maniac to embark on his killing sprees.

Hanks worked three days on the quickie feature, which resulted in seven minutes of screen time for him. Of his moviemaking debut, he admits, "I didn't know what I was doing. I just showed up and learned how to hit a mark [a spot identified on the floor of the set by chalk marks or bits of masking tape to establish an actor's position for the upcoming camera shot]." In the haphazard plot Hanks's character appears, talks about the killer's psychological makeup, and then disappears from the narrative. Years later Tom laughingly bemoaned, "I don't even get killed [in the story]."

He Knows You're Alone was released without fanfare in September 1980. Tom Buckley (*New York Times*) described the entry as "the latest in a ghoul's parade of cheaply made horror movies." The critic for the *Los Angeles Times* complained, "That people should pay money to see such films is ridiculous when you think about it." *He Knows You're Alone* came and went quickly at the theatrical box office. Years later it would reemerge in VHS format for the home entertainment marketplace.

California Bound

Now that Hanks's career was on an upswing of sorts, he and Samantha decided to formalize their relationship. On January 4, 1980, they married in the Church of the Holy Apostles in New York City. Their young son, Colin, ran about the church during the ceremony.

Meanwhile Tom had a feature-film credit—from a major studio—for his acting resume. Tom's representatives now touted this role to casting agents, which led to job auditions in New York. This, in turn, paved the way for interest among West Coast casting agents. Before long 23-year-old Hanks was scraping together funds to fly to Los Angeles, as his agency had lined up auditions for him there.

Bright-eyed and still naive, Tom arrived at his representatives' West Coast office wearing a sweat suit. His dismayed agent quickly handed him a few hundred dollars to buy more appropriate outfits for making crucial casting rounds. A key appointment for Tom was at ABC-TV, where the network had a talent program geared to discovering fresh personalities for the company's upcoming shows.

When Hanks appeared for his appointment with Joyce Selznick and Jan McCormack, who were then in charge of ABC's talent development program, he already had a knack for good auditions. Having been rejected at so many past tryouts, Tom had developed a protective feeling of indifference toward these casting sessions. This can be a good attitude for actors as it helps them overcome nervousness about such meetings and enables them to be casual and spontaneous. To further prepare for such encounters, Tom constantly reminded himself he was "just as good as 50 percent of the competition. And I believed that I was better than 45 percent of the competition. So that meant if the remaining 5 percent, who are gifted geniuses that I cannot touch in a million years, if they just don't happen to show up for an audition, I've got a shot. I might just get lucky."

Years later Jan McCormack could still recall meeting Hanks for his ABC tryout. "Tom came in, and there was a couch in the room. And he did a flip over it, like he tripped. And you just said, 'Wow.' So we were having him read for comedy. And then we asked him for serious. And he just went right into it. That was a young Jack Lemmon [an established, Oscar-winning star]."

As a result of the awesome impression he made at ABC on return visits, Hanks was signed to a $50,000 agreement that gave the network a year to cast him in one of its TV series. This "holding" contract allowed Tom's agents to negotiate other types of projects elsewhere, such as feature films, made-for-TV movies, TV specials, and so on. Hoping to quickly utilize its new employee, ABC auditioned Hanks for several of its shows. This resulted in Hanks being cast for an episode of the long-running series *The Love Boat*. Tom showed up on the "Friends and Lovers" episode, which aired October 25, 1980. It would be a satisfying experience for Hanks and his family to watch his small-screen debut.

Meanwhile, almost out of the blue, he received a call from ABC executives regarding one of their new TV programs for the 1980 fall season. The half-hour series was titled *Bosom Buddies*, and Tom was being considered to play one of the leads. He found the turn of events pretty amazing, since he had not even auditioned for the project. Looking back the star would say, "I had no idea what I was getting into. If somebody had told me, I would have probably choked."

Acting in a Dress

Bosom Buddies had been packaged by the seasoned executive producers Edward K. Milkis, Thomas L. Miller, William Boyett, and Chris Thompson. They had been involved with popular TV shows such as *Laverne & Shirley*. The new offering was a comedy involving the old routine of two guys disguised as women. This gimmick, for example, had been used successfully in the 1959 movie *Some Like It Hot*.

The story line for *Bosom Buddies* concerns two young New York ad agency hotshots who share an apartment.

When their decrepit building is demolished and they are desperately seeking new living quarters, one of their office coworkers suggests they move into her building. The only problem is that it's an all-female residence. Nevertheless, inspired by the low rent and the potential of being around beautiful, young women, the two men follow through on the wild notion. Pretending to be their own sisters, they dress as females and are allowed to move into the Susan B. Anthony Hotel for Women.

From left to right: Tom, Wendie Jo Sperber, and Peter Scolari in an episode of Bosom Buddies. (Photofest)

ABC originally had pursued two other actors for the sitcom, but when those pursuits did not work out, the producers turned to Peter Scolari and Tom Hanks. Twenty-six-year-old Scolari had been featured in a recently canceled ABC series *Goodtime Girls*. He was given the lead role (and top billing) on *Bosom Buddies* as Henry Desmond, the junior copywriter who aspires to be a novelist. Tom auditioned and was cast at the last minute as Kip Wilson, a fledgling illustrator who hopes to become a painter. The pilot was shot and picked up for distribution by Paramount TV.

ABC scheduled *Bosom Buddies* to air on Thursday nights, sandwiched between two of its established comedy properties: *Mork & Mindy* and *Barney Miller*. As such, much of the audience who tuned in for those popular shows stayed on that channel to sample *Bosom Buddies* when it premiered on November 27, 1980. The new entry achieved decent home viewer ratings, which soon guaranteed it would last the season. The trade paper *Variety* was not fond of the unoriginal premise. However, it gave the show a qualified thumbs up, reasoning, "The key to this kind of humor is the flair of the performers—and Peter Scolari and Tom Hanks get a good chemistry going between them, buttressed by fine timing for young players."

With his acting background largely in Shakespearean stage work, Hanks initially had qualms about handling a TV production. Like Scolari, Tom was apprehensive about appearing in female disguise each week, especially since—even with full makeup on—he looked too masculine to be a convincing woman. The costars soon discovered that their makeovers for each new episode were a painfully tedious chore, and one that might soon wear out its welcome with the public. Nevertheless, they gave the show their best efforts.

Recalling *Bosom Buddies,* Hanks acknowledged, "Everyone was trying to prove himself. It took a season for it to be fun, for me to realize that—at the core—it was the same process [as doing theater]. . . . There was a lot of insecurity." While being trained on the job, the TV rookie Hanks learned that giving a television performance differed from doing stage work. He found out that "the camera does a lot of the work for you. That you don't have to yell so loud. . . . And you don't have to be hyperactive. . . . I began to listen to people's subtle hints to shut up."

Costarring in *Bosom Buddies* sharpened other aspects of Tom's acting skills. "It made us very fast. The whole thing was delivering the goods as best you could. If you couldn't deliver them good, you had to deliver them bad, as long as you delivered them. It's flying by the seat of your pants. You ask as many questions as you can, but eventually it's 'Never mind, just do it.' You can't be lazy. It became our whole life. . . . It was a dense, dense time."

During their debut season on *Bosom Buddies,* Tom and Peter became good friends as they bulldozed their way through the often-trite weekly plots; they frequently ad-libbed to give the show more spark, zip, and originality. Since Tom and his family were now living near Scolari in the San Fernando Valley outside Los Angeles, the two twentysomething actors commuted to work together daily. On the trip to the TV soundstage, Tom and Peter worked up routines for their on-camera shenanigans.

By the time *Bosom Buddies* completed its first season, in the spring of 1981, the network gave a green light (an industry term meaning a go-ahead) to the show for a second season that fall. By then Tom was earning $9,000 an episode, which allowed him to repay the money he borrowed when he first moved to Los Angeles. When the sitcom returned to the air in October 1981, ABC decreased the then tiresome female drag routine and allowed Hanks and Scolari to caper more often as fast-witted, creative guys on the hunt for beautiful women. Unfortunately the

Although Bosom Buddies *lasted only a few seasons, it helped launch Tom's professional career. In the final season of the show, Tom rarely appeared in women's clothes.* (Photofest)

network lost faith in the series, as demonstrated by its constant switching of the show's broadcast time on the program schedule. Even faithful viewers of *Bosom Buddies* were annoyed trying to figure out when the comedy would be broadcast.

Having aired a total of 38 *Bosom Buddies* episodes, ABC canceled the series in the spring of 1982. Like most of the cast, Tom was not sorry to see the program end. They were all exhausted from the pressured production schedule and felt the comedy's premise had worn itself out. It was just around this time of being freed from the weekly grind that Samantha gave birth to the Hanks' second child, Elizabeth, on May 17, 1982.

Seeking New Career Horizons

According to Hanks's ABC deal, he was to appear in episodes of the network's other ongoing TV series. He was a guest on *Taxi* in the spring of 1982 and, that fall, was in an episode of *Happy Days*. In the latter, he played the wimp-turned-karate-expert classmate of the Fonz (played by Henry Winkler). In addition Hanks performed on two episodes of the comedy *Family Ties*. He was cast as the alcoholic younger brother of Meredith Baxter-Birney's character.

In a more important career move, Hanks gained a lead role in a two-hour TV movie, *Rona Jaffe's "Mazes and Monsters."* The telefeature was based on Jaffe's best-selling

1981 novel and was shot in Canada. It presented Tom as a college student who became so immersed in a role-playing game (modeled after Dungeons & Dragons) that he literally lost himself in it, striving to outwit rivals and survive elaborate obstacles. The film and novel were based on a real-life incident.

As Tom would do with many later acting assignments, he based his characterization on personal experience. He explained, "I had a perception of the game that people who haven't played it wouldn't have. If you have a particularly vivid imagination, it can be quite scary. The deeper, darker demons we all have inside us can really come to the forefront." For Tom, this assignment was quite an acting challenge. "I have to let Tom Hanks disappear into the background when the cameras roll. But that is what is the most fun about it. I feel I'm working at a much more intense level than . . . at various times in the past."

Tom (second from left) received favorable reviews for his appearance in the TV film Rona Jaffe's "Mazes and Monsters." (Photofest)

When *Rona Jaffe's "Mazes and Monsters"* aired on CBS on December 28, 1982, it received respectable viewership ratings. The *New York Times* said that "the younger actors [in the cast] are required to carry the film and they do so with remarkable skill." *Variety* rated Hanks's performance a "solid turn."

Facing an Uncertain Future

Like most artists, actors can never count on having a stable career and income. After being a television series costar, Hanks was now on his own, scrambling for guest assignments on other people's shows. His insecurities kicked in and, once again, he doubted his future in show business. Adding to his professional concerns were growing tensions in the Hanks' household. Now the mother of two, Samantha felt frustrated that her career ambitions as a performer and producer were being stifled and sacrificed for Tom's ambitions. The friction between the couple continued to grow. Falling back on childhood patterns, when Tom had put his difficult home life out of mind as much as possible, he did the same with his troubled marriage. He found the best remedy for his problems was to bury himself in work. The problem was that acting assignments were still few and, to his mind, too far between.

Then a screenplay about a mermaid entered his life and changed his career forever.

4

SPLASHING INTO SUCCESS

By the time that Tom Hanks had appeared in a 1982 episode of *Happy Days,* Ron Howard, who played the central character of Richie Cunningham, had left the long-running TV show to pursue a career in film directing. However, Howard still watched the weekly sitcom and had been impressed with Hanks's guest performance. In addition he still played on the *Happy Days* baseball team and met Tom, who joined in for some games. Howard could tell that Tom had a reservoir of talent waiting to be fully tapped.

Later, having successfully directed the comedic feature *Night Shift* (1982), Howard was preparing a new screen project, *Splash* (1984), with his producing partner Brian Grazer. The film had already suffered setbacks. It was initially planned as a United Artists release, but that company had dropped the film because of rumors that another studio was planning a similar-themed project (which never happened). Later *Splash* caught the attention of people at Disney, who thought the love story of a mermaid and a young man would make a good debut entry for Touchstone Pictures, Disney's newly established division to produce films for older audiences. Disney provided an $8 million budget for *Splash*.

Because of the threat of a film actors' strike, the *Splash* team was under pressure to complete casting and start shooting before the projected walkout occurred. Comedian John Candy, a star of television's *SCTV*, was being considered for one of the two leading male characters, who are brothers in the film. However, the filmmakers were having trouble finding the right performer to play the other brother. Dudley Moore, Chevy Chase, Bill Murray, and John Travolta, among others, were either unavailable or had turned down the part. Eventually the *Splash* team turned to the current crop of TV names for likely candidates. In the process Howard remembered Hanks and brought him in to audition. Said Howard, "He read, and he was terrific. We just stopped looking."

During the audition process the filmmakers realized that Tom, originally considered to play the obnoxious Freddie, had the dramatic range and warmth to handle the role of the brother Allen Bauer. Allen is the idealistic hero who finds it difficult to commit to a romantic relationship. In the film he reencounters a mermaid whom he first met when he was a child. Allen realizes it has been his long-standing love for this unusual creature that has prevented him from falling in love with anyone else.

With Tom set for a key role, Candy was switched to the part of the womanizing Freddie. The beautiful blond actress Daryl Hannah, a relative unknown, was cast as the mermaid. Before actual filming began Tom, Daryl, and the crew underwent rigorous underwater training. At the end of 16 days of instruction, according to Tom, "I was a certified diver. Not that there was any danger. We weren't really diving in more than 40 feet of water. In fact, it was kind of fun—for me. I'm sure it wasn't fun for Daryl. She had that fin on her!"

Working in the Deep

The underwater preparation was for the movie's aquatic scenes that were shot in the Bahamas as well as in studio tanks. For those sequences Hanks and Hannah had to work submerged without oxygen tanks. In the difficult process they filmed an undersea sequence, then hastily swam to a nearby lifeline to suck in breaths of air. Because it was impossible to talk—let alone be heard—underwater, the actors and technicians developed a set of hand signals to communicate with one another when submerged.

For the scenes on dry land, Hanks learned several useful acting lessons that helped him vary his comedic acting

Tom and Daryl Hannah share an underwater kiss in Splash. *Both actors had to undergo extensive underwater training for the film.* (Photofest)

style. Developing this sort of range is of great benefit to an actor. Howard cautioned Tom, "Your job is not to go toe-to-toe with John Candy and get laughs. If you do that, this movie will stink. Your job is just to love the girl. Just look at her and love her." The director further explained, "If we don't believe this girl is magic to you, we don't have a movie." Once Hanks adjusted to the demands, he had a new point of view toward his screen role. "I was never saying, 'Let's do this 'cause it would be funny,'" says Hanks. "I was saying, 'Let's do this because it would be interesting.' It would fill the guy out a bit." Compared to his unsubtle comedic acting on *Bosom Buddies*, Hanks learned to tone down his performance for *Splash*. He had to allow the comedy to come more from his reactions than from broad physical actions. During the shoot Tom displayed a keen knack for improvising, which greatly impressed Ron Howard.

Of even greater importance, making *Splash* taught Hanks humility and responsibility. At one point, Hanks had not paid sufficient attention to the daily call sheet, which detailed the schedule for the next day's shoot. As a result, one morning Tom arrived on the set less prepared than he should have been. Hanks remembers, "There was a scene with a huge plot point and a huge character point, and it caught me by surprise. . . . We did it again and again. Eventually, we got it. . . . Ron was calm. But he summed up the whole experience by telling me, 'It would have been nice if you were a little more prepared today.'" It was a vital lesson Hanks never forgot. Profiting from his professional misstep, Hanks went on to forge a great working and personal rapport with Howard. Besides enabling him to grow as an actor, *Splash* helped Tom in other ways: It encouraged his enthusiasm for scuba diving, and his salary from the film enabled him to purchase a reflector telescope to further pursue his interest in astronomy and outer space.

When *Splash* debuted in March 1984 it was an immediate hit with moviegoers. The critics were also enthusiastic.

Variety reported, "Hanks makes a fine leap from sitcom land." *New York* magazine's David Denby was particularly upbeat about Tom's screen potential, rating Hanks an expert comic who is "good-looking and relaxed enough to be a leading man." Denby added, "He commands the emotional center of the scenes, holding your sympathy in place." *Splash* went on to gross more than $69 million in domestic distribution. Tom was ecstatic: "That's a lot of money. You can't get much better right out of the box. It's perfect."

Invitation to a Bachelor Party

While *Splash* was in postproduction in late 1983 and no one knew what a hit it would become, Tom signed on for the film *Bachelor Party* (1984). It was a crude movie comedy about a wild night for a bewildered young school-bus driver about to get married. The comedy had already been shooting at Twentieth Century-Fox for a few days when the producers realized that Paul Reiser and Kelly McGillis were miscast in the leads. In a last-minute rush Hanks and Tawny Kitaen were hired as replacements. Hanks was suggested for the role by Wendie Jo Sperber, a *Bachelor Party* cast member who had been a regular on *Bosom Buddies*.

Tom had initial reservations about this film, as he wondered "what the challenge was going to be." This time, with the approval of director Neal Israel and the producers, he took a more active role in making the story come to life. In the process he helped to tone down, to a degree, some of the cruder aspects of the R-rated feature. He reasoned, "I wasn't interested in throwing myself at a wall or dropping my pants. We needed to get something better." What appealed to him about the project, besides his $60,000 fee, was a particular theme of the movie. "I thought it said something about fidelity in life today," said Hanks.

Bachelor Party was released in June 1984, three months after *Splash*. The talented cast overcame much of the plot's silly humor. In his nice-guy guise, Tom was applauded by *Variety* for his "overabundance of energy." Despite her reservations about this lowbrow screen fare, Janet Maslin of the *New York Times* pointed out, "Mr. Hanks's suave smart-alecky manner owes a lot to [TV and screen comedian] Bill Murray, but he's funny and engaging even if he isn't doing anything new." *Bachelor Party* proved to be a summer hit, grossing $38.4 million in domestic distribution.

The Workaholic Young Star

With two box-office successes to his credit, Hanks was becoming a known commodity in Hollywood. Increasingly, he became the subject of media interest. For example, the press wondered why he had participated in such a lowbrow film as _Bachelor Party_. He answered, "I'm an actor. An actor has to act. What else am I supposed to do—sit around the house?"

Ironically, under ordinary circumstances, that is just what Tom enjoyed doing most. On one occasion he revealed, "I just like to piddle around. I talk on the phone, watch television, read, and that's about it. I like boredom—I save the exciting stuff for work." However, the continuing dissension between Hanks and his wife— which he kept carefully masked from the world—colored his time at home, affecting his potential enjoyment of being a family man with two youngsters. It led Tom to grab every reasonable movie assignment offered, especially those that took him on location and away from his wife with whom he shared so few interests.

In this emotional state Hanks rushed off to Washington, D.C., to star in _The Man with One Red Shoe_ (1985). The spy spoof was a remake of an earlier French feature that had been successful in Europe. For his role as a concert violinist suddenly caught up in CIA activities, Tom devoted many hours to learning the mechanics of playing the instrument. He was determined that on camera his fingering and bowing would look believable, since the actual sounds of his violin were dubbed by a professional musician. Despite the efforts of Tom and coplayers such as Jim Belushi and Carrie Fisher, this screen satire was a bust. In retrospect Hanks rates this as the worst film of his career.

Without a breather Tom started work on *Volunteers* (1985), which was shot in Mexico. This comedic film, set in 1962, reunited him with John Candy. In *Volunteers* Hanks plays Lawrence Bourne III, a snobbish Yale graduate with an oversized gambling habit. To escape unhappy creditors, Lawrence stands in for his roommate as a Peace Corps volunteer sent to Thailand. There, as a member of the U.S. government's goodwill team, he is stuck with a group of idealistic, naive souls determined to "save" the civilian population by making them more like Americans. Dispatched to a small native village, Tom's self-centered character is at odds with well-meaning Beth Wexler (played by Rita Wilson) as the duo joins forces to save the locals from a vicious warlord. Eventually awakening to his responsibilities to fellow human beings, Hanks's reluctant hero discovers his compassionate side and, in the process, wins Beth's love.

Hanks's latest screen role enabled him to explore a multifaceted character who is both a glib, cynical aristocrat and a blossoming hero. Tom admitted that his *Volunteers* part was "the first job I've had where the gut instinct was not all that was necessary." To gain the proper diction to portray the urbane playboy, the actor worked with a dialogue coach. In addition Hanks, a casual—almost sloppy—

dresser in real life, was guided by the film's costume designer regarding his upscale wardrobe.

Despite Tom's misgivings about the *Volunteers* role, he proved adept during filming. Later, Nicholas Meyer, the picture's director, would say, "He was always very professional; there was nothing you could fault; he would do anything you'd ask him, but he wasn't prepared to reveal himself as a human being." If Hanks maintained an invisible emotional shield toward most people on the set, he somewhat let down his guard with his leading lady. He found he had a great rapport with the 26-year-old Wilson. Born Margarita Ibrahimoff in Los Angeles, Wilson was the daughter of a Greek mother and a Bulgarian father.

Tom, Rita Wilson, and John Candy in Volunteers. (Photofest)

Rita had modeled since childhood. Later she did TV commercials and studied acting for a year at London's Academy of Music and Dramatic Art. She had been in a few TV movies and features before being cast in *Volunteers*. In fact, in 1981 she had guest starred on an episode of Hanks's sitcom *Bosom Buddies*, although she and Tom had shared little on-screen time during that segment. Now in Mexico making *Volunteers*, Hanks found Wilson to be "amazingly cool, not cocky." The two spent a good deal of time together on and off the set. However, their relationship remained platonic because Rita was involved with someone back in Los Angeles and Tom was still unhappily married to Samantha.

Volunteers was released in August 1985. Reviewers complained that the film was an uneasy blend of slapstick comedy, satire, idealism, romance, and drama. Nonetheless, Hanks received some good notices, such as with *Newsweek*'s David Ansen, who said, "His character requires both the outside smirk of a Bill Murray and the debonair inside moves of a Cary Grant, and Hanks has both."

Fighting an Uphill Battle

Tom remained in his Cary Grant mode for *The Money Pit* (1985), a remake of Grant's 1948 comedy hit, *Mr. Blandings Builds His Dream House*. In this broad farce Tom and his screen wife (played by Shelley Long of TV's *Cheers*) are two New Yorkers who move to the country. They quickly discover that their spacious new home requires a tremendous amount of expensive and time-consuming repairs. While coping with various renovation catastrophes, the couple's marriage almost ends. By this point Hollywood had discovered that regardless of the type or caliber of film in which Hanks appeared, he was an incredibly likable actor to whom audiences responded heartily. Thus, despite several artistic misfires, Tom's asking fee per movie kept mounting. For *The Money Pit*, he received a $750,000 salary. And he earned it.

Hanks's screen role called for great physical agility as he undertook pratfalls, was covered in plaster, and ducked an amazing array of flying objects on the construction-site set. Making matters worse, such arduous scenes often had to be repeated several times to capture all the right elements on film. Despite the physical toll of such stunts, Tom's adventurous inner child responded to the arduous challenges of the role. "I look at it this way: There's an element of danger that you don't find in most professions. I like being the only member on the set who is not wearing a protective face shield during the shot."

Made at a cost of $10 million, *The Money Pit* grossed $37.5 million in domestic distribution. With too many predictable sight gags, it is not a picture that most moviegoers remember fondly.

Tom's next film was *Nothing in Common* (1986), which he chose to make for many reasons. First, it gave him an opportunity to costar with Jackie Gleason, the veteran stage, TV, and film comedian who had demonstrated his impressive acting abilities in such features as *The Hustler* (1961). For another, Hanks would get to work again with veteran director and producer Garry Marshall, who had helmed Tom's *Happy Days* TV appearance a few years earlier. Finally, this new project allowed the rising star to combine comedy and drama on camera. Hanks felt he was now seasoned enough to tackle a demanding assignment that required him to "tone it down, rein it in, and start trying to tell the truth, as opposed to just telling a joke."

Even more important to Hanks than his impressive $1 million fee for the film (part of a three-movie development pact with Columbia Pictures) was that he felt personally invested in the picture's story line. *Nothing in Common* revolves around a long-married couple (Gleason and Eva Marie Saint) who decide to divorce. Thereafter Gleason loses his job and ends up in the hospital with serious diabetic problems. This series of family crises forces Tom's character, the couple's son who is a cocky advertising executive, to reevaluate his detached approach to life and to really come to know and appreciate his parents in their time of difficulty. These plot lines mirrored Tom's real-life relationship with his father, Amos, who had been suffering from severe kidney problems for many years and had nearly died on several occasions. In the 1980s Amos underwent two kidney transplant operations, but his health remained precarious. The ongoing situation brought father and son much closer together after years of only fleeting communication.

Moviegoers were puzzled by the uneasy blend of comedy and drama within *Nothing in Common,* and it fared only moderately well at the box office. Nevertheless, Hanks was glad he made the venture, which demonstrated his versatility as an actor. The *Los Angeles Times'*

In Nothing in Common, *Tom took on a complex dramatic role and worked with Hollywood legend Jackie Gleason.* (Photofest)

reviewer complimented Tom for his ability to "sustain beautifully a growing seriousness."

Box Office Fodder

Meanwhile, in 1986, *Every Time We Say Goodbye*, another of Tom's pictures, was released briefly. Set in Jerusalem during World War II, it was a love tale between an American pilot and a young Jewish woman. The poorly conceived Tri-Star movie played in very few U.S. theaters.

Much more high profile was Hanks's participation in *Dragnet* (1987), an elaborate movie spoof of the classic TV police series, which aired in the 1950s and 1960s. Tom, who wanted to work with Dan Aykroyd, agreed to take a secondary role in the Universal production. He was cast as Aykroyd's unorthodox Los Angeles Police Department partner. Because Dan played his role extremely deadpan, Tom had to tone down his slapstick performance as a sloppy, trouble-prone, undercover cop. Unfortunately Hanks's character came across as tedious and one-dimensional, as did most of the film, according to responses from many critics and audiences. As such, the expensive picture did poorly.

In relatively few years Tom had played a key role in eight features, many of which were commercial and/or artistic disappointments. He began to wonder if both his marriage and career were headed for failure.

5

HITTING THE BIG TIME

In 1985 only a few people close to Tom Hanks knew that he had moved out of his North Hollywood home. The problems between he and his wife, Samantha, had accelerated as his acting career had jumped ahead, and she was depressed in her role as a housewife. Tom's absence from home while making movies nonstop fueled the growing rift between him and Samantha.

Tom felt most guilty about the little time he had spent with his two young children. For Hanks, fatherhood had passed like a blur, and most of that time he had chosen to be away on filming locations. Tom tried to repair his marriage by supporting his wife's efforts to reactivate her acting career, helping her when she produced and starred in a stage production. But their marital difficulties seemed past the point of resolution. As the situation worsened the couple recognized that divorce was their only solution.

Having reached that conclusion, Hanks came to a disturbing realization: "Oh my God; my kids are going to feel as lonely as I did [as a child]."

While Tom and Samantha were undergoing the painful divorce procedures, he and Rita Wilson began dating and appearing together at industry functions.

After months of bitter haggling over custody of their two children, who went to Samantha, and a financial division of their assets, Tom and Samantha were officially divorced in 1987. So that his children would not feel abandoned, Tom made every effort to remain part of their lives, often taking them on location for his latest movie, as well as attending important milestones in their lives.

As to Hanks's relationship with his ex-wife, he would acknowledge later, "Their mother and I don't talk a lot any more, but we're very respectful of each other. I wouldn't say we're friends, or even friendly. But we are very respectful of each other's

Rita Wilson and Tom were married in 1988. (Photofest)

place and position." After the divorce Samantha and the two children relocated to northern California.

On New Year's Eve of 1987 Tom asked Rita Wilson to marry him. Her answer was a jubilant "You bet!" To please Rita, Tom became a member of the Greek Orthodox Church. The couple wed on April 30, 1988, in Los Angeles in a big ceremony filled with family and friends. The newlyweds honeymooned in the Caribbean.

Big Changes

Even during this time of great change in his personal life, Tom continued his hectic moviemaking pace. When first Harrison Ford, then Warren Beatty, and next Robert De Niro dropped out of the starring role in *Big* (1988), director Penny Marshall (the sister of filmmaker Garry Marshall) turned to her friend Hanks. She asked him to star in this screen comedy cowritten by Anne Spielberg, the sister of filmmaker Steven Spielberg. Tom quickly accepted the role at a $1.75 million fee. Hanks liked the project, saying, "What I dug about it was there was no car chases, no bad guys, no guns. A massive amount of the movie is just two people sitting around talking."

Big is the story of a 12-year-old boy who makes a wish to become a grown-up. The next morning he awakens to find that he is a 35-year-old man, and no one will believe his explanation about the abrupt change. Later he gets a job with a large toy company, and is soon promoted to an executive position. At the firm he meets a beautiful employee (Elizabeth Perkins). Won over by his boyish charm, she quickly falls in love with him. Toward the end of the movie the hero realizes he misses being a teenager, and maneuvers to have the wish-granting machine transform him back into a youth.

In *Big* Tom embraced his inner child—with great results. To play the child effectively, the star had to undergo a tough process: "It required a lot of paring back of the stuff I'd done before, and done with some success. This is a guy who isn't very verbal or aggressive. I've played guys who

Robert Loggia (left) and Tom in Big*'s famous piano scene.*
(Photofest)

were verbal, aggressive, sarcastic, and caustic. In this case, I had to play someone who is literally innocent." Although Tom grew impatient with Penny Marshall's habit of endlessly rehearsing scenes, he discovered that the process actually was extremely useful. The method gave the actor tremendous confidence in his knowledge of a scene, providing him the assurance to improvise creatively within the confines of his character.

Released in June 1988 *Big* won great endorsements from the media. Gerald Clark from *Time* magazine applauded, "Hanks, who emerges from this film as one of Hollywood's top comic actors, is both believable and touching as a boy lost in a grown-up world." The *New York Times*' Janet Maslin confirmed, "Mr. Hanks is an absolute delight." Made at a cost of $18 million, *Big* grossed $115 million in domestic distribution. For his performance Tom was nominated for a Best Actor Academy Award, a prize he lost to Dustin Hoffman for Hoffman's performance in *Rain Man*.

Punchline (1988), which was made before but released after *Big*, is a story about a housewife and mother (played by Sally Field) who dreams of becoming a stand-up comic. At an amateur night competition she encounters Steven Gold (played by Hanks)—a brilliant, biting, rising comic. Soon she is relying on him for career guidance and the two develop romantic feelings for one another. At a televised competition the duo compete for a chance to appear on a major TV program. By then Field's character has had to choose between staying with her husband or going with Hanks's character, the latter a sad man haunted by emotional demons from his past.

Punchline presented two major artistic challenges for Hanks: First, he had to interpret a rather nasty individual and second, he had to perform actual stand-up comedy routines. Tom was particularly nervous about performing stand-up—something he had always strenuously avoided because he felt it lay beyond his abilities. However, he knew that facing up to this artistic risk would make him a better all-around performer. David Seltzer, the film's writer and director, encouraged Hanks to perform in actual comedy clubs and develop his own stand-up material. The resultant routine could be utilized within the movie and, in the process, would give the actor insights into his characterization. Regarding the trying process Hanks said, "Eventually, after the entire course of shooting [*Punchline*], I had a 40-minute act. We had a bona fide stand-up comedy presentation that was funny unto itself. So in doing that, it was more preparatory activity than just research. This was a life experience."

Although it was released in September 1988, after *Big*'s success, *Punchline* did not benefit from the acclaim given Hanks in *Big*. Many reviewers thought *Punchline* was an awkward mix of comedy and drama, and that its romantic themes were underdeveloped. Made at a cost of $15 million, *Punchline* only grossed $21 million in domestic distribution. Although disappointed by the lukewarm reaction of the public and critics, Tom had no regrets about making this entry. In 1989 Hanks said, "It's the best work I've ever done. We were talking some real naked truths about the characters and, in a lot of ways, about myself." These truths included Hanks's own inability to balance properly his work and private life and to temper his highly competitive nature.

Stuck in a Career Rut

Much in demand after the success of *Big*, Hanks was now receiving major film offers on a daily basis. In selecting among the scripts he received, Tom turned down lead assignments in much-praised films such as *Dead Poets Society* and *Field of Dreams*. Instead he made *The 'burbs*, a wacky story that satirized suburban life. Teamed with Carrie Fisher as his wife and Bruce Dern as one of his bizarre neighbors, the story involves suburbanites investigating the spooky house of a strange family who has moved into their tight-knit neighborhood. The film was a black comedy that was part social satire and part horror spoof, but it never focused on either genre effectively. Even Hanks, Hollywood's most likable new star, received a critical roasting for his performance as a house owner on the verge of a nervous breakdown. Richard Corliss (*Time*) complained, "Hanks throws himself into this antiaudience movie with such suave energy that he seems determined to torpedo his hard-won rep as Hollywood's most comfortable new star."

As part of a new pact with the Disney studio, Tom next starred in *Turner & Hooch* (1989). It was a buddy comedy that teamed him with one of the ugliest pooches in cinema. Tom's role in the film required that he spend a lot of time bonding with his canine costar before production began.

While certainly not one of Tom's more challenging assignments—or a film that he is particularly proud of—*Turner & Hooch* did quite well at the box office, grossing $71.1 million in domestic distribution. The picture's director, Roger Spottiswoode, said of Tom's dedication throughout the shoot: "I never worked with an actor who is as much a film-maker and who takes a great deal of responsibility for the film without being an interferer."

In 1989 Tom returned to TV's *Saturday Night Live* (which he had hosted on past occasions) to participate in the variety show's 15th anniversary special.

An Offbeat Entry

Next Hanks was cast as a hypochondriac in *Joe Versus the Volcano* (1990), an unusual romantic comedy produced by Steven Spielberg's Amblin Entertainment. Tom played a meek clerk named Joe who is full of imaginary ailments. After seeing a doctor who diagnosed him with a fatal disease, Tom's character agreed to an eccentric billionaire's unusual offer: enjoy his remaining time in lavish fashion in exchange for making a human sacrifice of himself at the end of this period to a volcano on a Polynesian island. Actress Meg Ryan played a trio of roles as Hanks's co-worker and the bizarre entrepreneur's two daughters.

From the start Tom realized that this unique screen fable might be a turnoff to moviegoers unless all the ingredients melded properly. Nevertheless he took a chance on starring in the risky property for a $3.5 million fee because, "I liked the emotional journey that Joe Banks [the lead character] was on." When released, *Joe Versus the Volcano* was a big disappointment, with first-time director John Patrick Shanley (who also wrote the script) receiving much of the blame.

The Bonfire of the Vanities and *Radio Flyer*

If *Joe Versus the Volcano* had been a misfire, it was nothing in comparison to *The Bonfire of the Vanities.* This project was based on Tom Wolfe's 1987 best-selling novel, a biting satire about race and class in 1980s New York City. The plot deals with a snobbish, self-indulgent Wall Street financier. His selfish life becomes a shambles when he and his mistress hit an African-American boy with their car in a dangerous south Bronx neighborhood. The police track down the rich man's vehicle and arrest its owner. The sensationalized trial that follows brings together a wide range of special interest groups who press for a conviction.

Warner Bros. had won the Hollywood bidding frenzy for the screen rights to *The Bonfire of the Vanities*. Then came a series of strange decisions regarding key assignments for the film. Surprisingly, Brian De Palma, noted for turning out film thrillers, was hired to direct the big-budget drama. Because the book had been so popular, there was much public interest in who would play the pivotal roles. Sterling actor William Hurt was a leading candidate for the part of Sherman McCoy, but De Palma insisted on Hanks in the assignment. The filmmaker reasoned, "I think Tom Hanks is the best comedic actor around who can convey a serous side. And there's no doubt in my mind that it's easier to play drama than it is to get that precise comic timing."

When offered the high-profile role, Hanks had initial concerns that he was not the ideal person to play the lead figure. Many of his inner circle agreed with his first reaction to the job offer. However, because this was such a major offer, Tom felt flattered to be asked to be part of it. He explained, "I wasn't about to say, 'Well, gee, I can't do the role.'" Hanks accepted the acting job for a $5 million salary.

The Bonfire of the Vanities was marked by several puzzling cast decisions. Melanie Griffith, noted more for her beauty than her acting abilities, was given the demanding role of Hanks's birdbrained lover. Smirky Bruce Willis, star of the action film *Die Hard* (1988), was cast as the disillusioned, alcoholic journalist who rebuilds his career reporting the big trial. Perhaps the biggest shock of all was in the choice of actor to play the film's spirited Jewish judge.

Kim Cattrall and Tom in The Bonfire of the Vanities. *This much-anticipated film was a box-office disappointment.* (Photofest)

After making failed bids for the services of either Walter Matthau or Alan Arkin, De Palma hired well-regarded African-American actor Morgan Freeman for the role. This casting decision required the rewriting of the film's plot to accommodate the change in the judge's ethnicity.

To research this pivotal role, Hanks spent time on Wall Street meeting with bond traders to learn what made them tick. As filming began in various parts of New York City, the star felt a bit overwhelmed by the sheer size of the elaborate production. It led Tom to wonder if the film was going to come together well.

Released during the Christmas season of 1990, *The Bonfire of the Vanities* was no holiday treat. Costing $47 million to make, the film grossed only $15.7 million in domestic distribution. It was soon labeled Hollywood's worst turkey of recent years.

In the aftermath of this box-office dud, the press repeatedly asked Hanks if he had not been aware during the shoot that things were going amiss. His response was, "It feels just the same when you're filming a hit or a flop." After the adverse public reaction to the picture, Tom tried to put *The Bonfire of the Vanities* out of mind. However, this was difficult to do, given all of the negative reviews in the media. Offsetting this career setback was the 1990 birth of Tom and Rita's son Chester.

Rounding out Hanks's streak of professional disappointments was *Radio Flyer*, filmed in the fall of 1990 but not released until early 1992. The offbeat story was a difficult blend of themes involving fantasy and child abuse. Tom, who chose not to be billed in the film's credits, narrates the tale as well as appearing briefly at the film's opening and closing. In the movie he relates to his young sons the strange events he and his brother experienced in his troubled childhood. The misguided picture also proved to be unsuccessful commercially.

At this time Hanks stepped back to reassess his screen career. Tom appreciated that too many of his 14 films from the past six years were not up to his personal standards. It led him, for a time, to withdraw from moviemaking in order to reevaluate his past method of choosing pictures he wanted to appear in. He realized that his approach to acting up to this point was flawed: "It became a matter of just getting it done, as opposed to doing it right," he said. With his life now suddenly freed of work commitments, he spent a good deal of time with his family, went surfing and skiing, and did his best to help his father during Amos's final years.

As Tom cleared his head and began to think again about his career, he also changed talent management. At this time he also met with his good friend Penny Marshall to ask if she would consider him for a part in her new picture, *A League of Their Own* (1992).

6

LIFE IS LIKE A BOX OF CHOCOLATES

When Tom Hanks took a nearly 19-month sabbatical from moviemaking he said, "It was the best thing for everybody. I needed a break from the industry. And the industry needed a little less of me for a while."

When Hanks returned to acting, he was determined to take only those screen parts that were challenging to him and meaningful to moviegoers. After signing with his new talent representation, the powerful Creative Artists, he told the agency that he now wanted to play stronger, more mature characters than he had in the past, characters that would complement his age and acting experience.

A League of Their Own

Before his time off from picturemaking, Hanks had been approached about taking a role in *A League of Their Own* (1992), a baseball story with a twist. The film dealt with the little-remembered women's professional teams that cropped up during World War II when most of the male players were serving in the war. Tom had initially rejected the role of the manager because it was not a starring part. Now, he went hat in hand to Penny Marshall, who had recently been signed to direct the period comedy. Because of Tom's string of recent high-profile flops and because he

Tom and actress Geena Davis in A League of Their Own. (Photofest)

typically played the leading man in movies, she was unsure that her friend was the right choice for the role of Jimmy Dugan—an overweight, alcoholic, former ball player who coaches the all-girls baseball team. Hanks said he was willing to do whatever it took to make Dugan, an unattractive personality, come to life. Marshall eventually agreed.

Hanks gained 30 pounds for this role. He also suggested giving his middle-aged character a limp (from an old sports injury) so audiences would not wonder why the coach remained a civilian during World War II. While Tom prepped for the role, Marshall assembled an intriguing cast, including Geena Davis, Madonna, and Rosie O'Donnell, to portray the baseball players.

Shot on location in Evansville, Indiana, *A League of Their Own* was released in midsummer 1992. The $40 million feature proved to be a huge crowd-pleaser, grossing $107 million in domestic distribution. Midst the praise for the film itself, Tom came in for a share of tributes. Vincent Canby of the *New York Times* judged, "With his work here, there can be no doubt that Mr. Hanks is now one of Hollywood's most accomplished and self-assured actors."

Hanks's gamble with *A League of Their Own* had paid off handsomely. Not only did he prove he had a far wider acting range than Hollywood insiders had imagined, but he also found a great deal of enjoyment in the offbeat role. As he joked, "The whole reason I did this movie was because it was going to be a blast. Come on, play baseball all summer with a bunch of girls? Please! Help me. And get paid for it? Fine. I'm there. When do we start?"

Sleepless in Seattle

Hanks considered *A League of Their Own* the start of his "modern era" of filmmaking in which he now focused on more genuine, dimensional parts. With this in mind he reteamed with Meg Ryan for *Sleepless in Seattle* (1993). This romantic love story would catapult the actor from the ranks of popular leading men to that of major Hollywood stars.

Directed by Nora Ephron (who contributed to the screenplay), *Sleepless in Seattle* was a glossy tearjerker that owed a great deal to *An Affair to Remember* (1957), which had costarred Cary Grant and Deborah Kerr. Hanks portrays a recent Seattle widower who, through a series of improbable and amusing events, ends up finding love in New York City with a woman he hardly knows (Meg Ryan) and never meets in person until the end of the film. Although Ryan and Hanks shared little actual screen time in *Sleepless in Seattle*, Meg was glad to work again with Tom. "He's able to find so much in a moment. . . . His work is very simple, and he always finds the strongest thing to do that says the most. There's something about him where you feel you can just fill in the blanks."

As Hollywood's favorite everyman, Tom has found much suc-cess in romantic comedies such as Sleepless in Seattle. *From left to right: Meg Ryan, Ross Malinger, and Hanks.* (Photofest)

With a domestic box-office gross of $127 million, *Sleepless in Seattle* was a huge hit. A good deal of the film's success was attributed to Hanks's Cary Grant-like performance. As one critic said, "The best reason to see [*Sleepless*] is Tom Hanks, but then he's always the best reason to see a movie."

Not only was Tom now back on top in Hollywood, but he was stretching his talents into other show-business arenas. He began directing episodes of TV series (including *Fallen Angels, Tales from the Crypt,* and a teleseries version of *A League of Their Own*). These assignments inspired Hanks to one day direct his own feature film.

Philadelphia

After British actor Daniel Day-Lewis proved unavailable for *Philadelphia* (1993), director Jonathan Demme turned to Tom Hanks to play the controversial lead part in this AIDS drama. According to Demme one of his main reasons for choosing Hanks was, "As a personality, Tom had the trust and confidence of Americans, which I felt would help us reach across to a mainstream audience." When Tom said yes to the role, he knew that he was taking a great career risk. He would be portraying Andrew Beckett, a successful attorney who is fired by his prestigious Pennsylvania law firm after it is discovered he has AIDS. In Hollywood at that time—and even today—there was a concern that if an actor portrayed a homosexual on-screen, he might "tarnish" his manly image and ruin his ability to be cast thereafter as a heterosexual leading man.

Hanks ignored those advisers who said he should turn down *Philadelphia*. He reasoned that his unusual childhood—full of sudden relocations and quickly changing family units—had made him appreciate what it was like to be an outsider. As the performer told CNN's Larry King, "I felt from the very beginning that I had an awful lot in common with the character of Andrew Beckett [in *Philadelphia*]. I thought that he was like me in so many aspects of my past and so many aspects of the way I look at life now. The fact that he was a gay man who was suffering from a terminal disease was, you know, in there, but I didn't see that as a massive obstacle."

To prepare for this challenging role, Tom conferred with medical specialists on the realities of AIDS. He also spoke with AIDS patients who explained the pains, fears, and discrimination they encountered as victims of this disease. In this difficult research process, Tom learned much about the disease and how it affects people's lives on many levels.

Tom said a very poignant moment occurred when he met with an AIDS patient who "told me that when he was first diagnosed, he went to the window and thought, 'Clouds, this is the last time I am going to see you.' I thought about that when I did one scene in the film and it brought tears to my eyes."

To gain visual believability as an AIDS patient, Hanks lost 30 pounds and had his hair increasingly

Tom won the Best Actor Academy Award for his performance as a man with AIDS in Philadelphia. (Photofest)

trimmed back throughout the filming. This, along with special makeup, helped him to achieve the emaciated look of a dying man. Hanks noted, "I'm not a big method actor. I don't immerse myself totally in a character. But I do end up being affected by all the stuff I do, and I found myself on this one crying over the most amazing and silly things."

When released, *Philadelphia* proved as controversial as expected. Many gay activist organizations felt that the feature film should have included more intimate moments between Hanks and his on-screen lover. Other such groups protested that the homosexual characters in the plot were too stereotypical. Despite these complaints, *Philadelphia*, made at a cost of $26 million, earned a worldwide gross of $201 million and touched audiences around the world. The *New York Times* said: "In the end, thanks to . . . the simple grace of Mr. Hanks's performance, this film does accomplish what it meant to. *Philadelphia* rises above its flaws to convey the full urgency of its difficult subject, and to bring that subject home."

On March 21, 1994, a proud, but bewildered, Tom Hanks walked onto the stage of the Dorothy Chandler Pavilion in Los Angeles to accept the Academy Award for Best Actor for his role in *Philadelphia*. Hanks received a standing ovation before he launched into a lengthy speech, in which he said, "My work is magnified by the fact that the streets of heaven are too crowded with angels—we know their names. They number a thousand for each of the red ribbons [the red lapel buttons signifying AIDS awareness] we wear here tonight."

Picking Another Winner

After the *Philadelphia* triumph Tom had little opportunity to relax and enjoy his domestic life, which now included homes in Los Angeles, Malibu, and New York City. He had already found a new film that captured his imagination: *Forrest Gump* (1994), based on a 1986 novel by Winston Groom. The story is about a simple but unique man with a modest IQ who experiences an amazing array of adventures over several years, including encounters with several U.S. presidents and other important world figures.

This offbeat fable was seen as risky because its main character was so different from the Hollywood movie norm. But Tom thought that the film and its uncomplicated, straightforward central character were very refreshing. Tom liked the character because of "the purity of how he sees the world." He signed on to the film, saying, "All the great stories are about our battle against loneliness. . . . That's what I always ended up being drawn to." Tom agreed to receive a percentage of the film's profits rather than accepting a straight salary. As a result of his gamble, the star eventually earned an estimated $60 million for this picture.

Released in the summer of 1994, _Forrest Gump_, directed by Robert Zemeckis for Paramount release, was a major hit. It earned a $674 million global gross on its $55 million cost. Much of the picture's praise was heaped on Hanks as the humble Gump, who mouths such famous lines as "Mama always said life was like a box of chocolates. You never know what you're gonna get."

Tom as Forrest Gump, the role for which he earned his second Academy Award. (Photofest)

So great was the _Forrest Gump_ phenomenon, which even inspired massive merchandizing tie-ins, that Hollywood observers felt that an aversion to the picture's overwhelming popularity might affect the film's chances in the upcoming Oscar race. On the contrary, the movie earned 13 Oscar nominations and won six Academy Awards, including Tom's second consecutive Best Actor award. At the ceremony, a beaming Hanks thanked his wife, Rita, who he said "has taught me and demonstrates to me every day just what love is."

With the public's mighty endorsement of *Forrest Gump*, Tom was now one of the movie industry's most powerful figures.

Heading to Outer Space

Since he was a child, Tom had been fascinated with America's space program. When he learned that his long-time friend Ron Howard was preparing the film *Apollo 13* (1995), Hanks was eager to land a part in the project and fulfill his boyhood fantasy of dressing up in astronaut gear. He excitedly told Howard that he would play any crewmember in the script. Howard signed two-time Oscar winner Hanks to enact Jim Lovell, a key astronaut aboard the spacecraft's aborted 1970 moon mission.

To research this major role, Tom spent time on land and in the skies (in a small aircraft) with the real Jim Lovell, a heroic man whom Hanks said "went through an almost superhuman experience." Tom also devoted much effort to reading the NASA transcripts of the real *Apollo 13* flight and any available background details on the near-fatal space trek.

By the time filming began on *Apollo 13,* Hanks was so well-prepared that Howard and his crew often called on the actor as their informal technical consultant. In fact, executive producer Brian Grazer pointed out, "Tom was at least 50 percent of the driving force of this movie. Because of his understanding of what actually happened on that mission, he was the truth meter of the movie. . . . Tom made it very clear how the tone [of the film] should be and helped police it."

Although *Apollo 13* was shot largely on studio soundstages, Howard utilized a real space simulator to create the zero-gravity aircraft in which the characters would be seen dealing with weightlessness in their dangerous outerspace flight. Such attention to detail gave added realism to this dramatic re-creation of the American craft.

The public responded heartily to this epic drama. *Variety* credited the picture as hitting "a commercial bull's-eye." *Time* magazine noted that Hanks "provides the anchor. His Lovell—as strong, faithful, and emotionally straightforward as Forrest Gump—carries the story like a precious oxygen backpack. His resourcefulness gives Lovell strength; his gift for conveying worry gives the film its humanity." Hanks's participation was worth the $17.5 million he was paid for *Apollo 13*, a film that grossed $334 million worldwide.

No Time to Breathe

In 1995 the ever-busy Hanks also participated in *The Celluloid Closet*, a documentary tracing the history of gay and lesbian characters and themes in American movies. In addition, that year Tom provided the voice of Woody, the old-fashioned toy cowboy in the computer-animated film *Toy Story*. Also in 1995, Tom and Rita welcomed their second son, Truman Hanks.

Having enjoyed directing TV episodes, Tom realized his interest of directing a feature film, *That Thing You Do!* (1996), in which he called upon his childhood memories and enthusiasm for the 1960s invasion of American music by British pop groups. The film focuses on a young group of small-town Pennsylvania musicians who, in 1964, rise to the top of the charts as one-hit wonders. The story then explores how their meteoric career break affects the group. Hanks wrote, produced, and directed the film, as well as played a small role and composed some of the film's songs.

While *That Thing You Do!* was a modest box-office success, working 18-hour days and seeing so little of his family convinced Tom to curtail his directing activities and return to acting. This led to Tom accepting an offer from longtime pal and Malibu Beach neighbor Steven Spielberg to star in a major World War II drama, *Saving Private Ryan* (1998).

LIVING AT THE TOP

When director Steven Spielberg was preparing *Saving Private Ryan*, his epic World War II drama, he wanted to depart from the Hollywood tradition of glamorizing combat on the screen. He intended to depict the hell of war in which there were no real victors. Hanks was in full agreement with Spielberg's point of view. As Tom pointed out to *People* magazine, "It's hard to understand the violence equation. That there are two sides to the equal sign—pull the trigger on a machine gun, make a loud glamorous noise and it's really fun; but on the other side of the equation is white-hot pieces of metal fly through people's flesh and make their skulls explode and they live no more. Or they're maimed forever. [Audiences] don't add the two pieces up."

Before filming of *Saving Private Ryan* began, Spielberg put his main cast through exhausting boot camp training. A retired Marine captain assigned to get the performers into shape for the rigorous location filming supervised them.

Set in 1944, the screen drama focuses on a U.S. Army squad led by Hanks's character, a former schoolteacher. They are ordered to work their way through German-occupied France to rescue a soldier whose three brothers have already been killed in combat; this soldier is to be sent home, sparing his family the loss of another son. In completing the dangerous mission, several squad members are killed by the enemy. Hanks's character, an ordinary man forced into difficult circumstances, finds irony in the fact that, to save one individual, others must die. However, he is duty-bound to follow through on his Army orders.

For many viewers the highlight of this lengthy feature was its graphic opening 20 minutes. In raw terms this footage revealed the nightmarish D-Day invasion on June 6, 1944, as Allied forces—including Hanks and his

Tom and Matt Damon in Saving Private Ryan. **(Photofest)**

men—land on the enemy-held Omaha Beach at Normandy. The bloodshed and gore shown in this gruesome sequence are unforgettable. Like the remainder of this realistic feature, this explicit segment shows the bravery of American soldiers fighting until death for a cause in which they believed wholeheartedly.

Saving Private Ryan registered strongly with reviewers, and Tom received much praise for his role as the commander. The *San Francisco Chronicle* said, "In an honest, foursquare performance, Hanks embodies the spirit of simple decency, one of the reasons for which the war was fought." The *Chronicle* reporter added, "In Hanks's performance, there is no doubt in my mind that he has taken the mantle of the quintessential American actor that once belonged to Jimmy Stewart."

Made for $70 million, *Saving Private Ryan* grossed $216 million in domestic distribution, with another $227.4 million grossed abroad. The picture received 11 Oscar nominations, including one for Hanks as Best Actor. Even though he had already won two Academy Awards, Tom was nervous about the awards ceremony. Although he lost the coveted prize to Italian performer Roberto Benigni, he was thrilled that moviegoers had responded so favorably to Spielberg's unglamorous depiction of warfare.

While making *Saving Private Ryan* Hanks learned of a campaign in the United States to raise funds to create a national memorial for those who served in World War II.

He so believed in the project that he volunteered his time to appear in filmed public-service ads to bring the fund-raiser to the public's attention.

Taking on New Challenges

It had now been five years since Hanks had appeared in a screen comedy. Ever the versatile actor, he decided to team up again with Meg Ryan for the 1998 romantic comedy *You've Got Mail*. In the film Hanks plays the successful owner of a bookstore chain who finds romance via e-mail with Ryan. She is the proprietor of a Manhattan neighborhood bookshop which Hanks's enterprise is threatening to shut down. In judging this highly popular screen entry, the *New York Times* acknowledged the special talents of the film's leading man by applauding Hanks's "romantic wistfulness," "poignant shyness," and his "lovely way of speaking from the heart."

While making his two 1998 film releases, Hanks also participated in *From the Earth to the Moon*, a 12-part HBO-cable series focusing on the Apollo space missions of the 1960s and 1970s. In addition to his producing chores on this daunting project, Tom wrote four of the segments, acted in the miniseries, and directed the first episode. As one of the project's several producers, Tom shared in the Emmy Award it won for Outstanding Miniseries.

Next Tom starred in *The Green Mile* (1999), a drama based on a six-part work of fiction by Stephen King. In the film Hanks plays the head guard on death row in a 1930s Louisiana penitentiary. Hanks's character comes to know one of the convicted men who, he discovers, has mystical healing powers. Once again Tom received many favorable reviews for his role in this fantastic tale.

Also in 1999 Tom revived his voice-over work for the character of Woody in *Toy Story 2.*

In April 1999 Tom was given a prestigious tribute by the American Museum of the Moving Image. More than 800 participants gathered at the Waldorf-Astoria Hotel in New York City to praise the 42-year-old Hanks. He was the youngest such recipient of the prize, as he was in 2002, when he received the American Film Institute's Lifetime Achievement honor.

Into the New Millennium

Tom Hanks reunited with *Forrest Gump* director Robert Zemeckis for *Cast Away* (2000), a picture released by Twentieth Century-Fox and DreamWorks, Steven Spielberg's new movie studio. The film, for which Tom supplied the basic plot idea and served as a producer, presented intriguing challenges for the now superstar actor. The plot called for Hanks's character to be stranded alone for four years on a remote Pacific island after his plane crashes. Rather than relying on makeup and special effects to show the radical changes between Hanks's character before and after the crash, it was decided that after the initial shoot on Fiji, Tom and the crew would return to Hollywood. Over the next several months Hanks underwent a severe diet, during which he lost more than 40 pounds, and grew a full beard. At that point the actor and crew returned to Fiji and filmed the rest of the movie.

For much of *Cast Away* Hanks is the sole performer on camera, depicting his routines of gathering food and trying to maintain his sanity and spirit throughout years of loneliness. Most of these sequences have no dialogue and the actor conveyed his emotions and reactions through gestures and looks. It takes a talented and well-liked actor

For his grueling role in Cast Away, *Tom lost 40 pounds.* (Photofest)

to hold an audience's attention through these kinds of scenes—which can become boring and predictable—and Tom did it well. Critics praised his performance, and the film did very well at the box office. Tom received his fifth Best Actor Oscar nomination for his role in *Cast Away,* but he lost to actor Russell Crowe.

Part of Tom's time away from the two-part *Cast Away* shoot was devoted to *Band of Brothers* (2001). This 10-episode, 600-minute miniseries for HBO was based on historian Stephen E. Ambrose's 1993 best-seller, which recounts the history of the 101 Airborne's Easy Company. The miniseries traces the company's harrowing combat experiences from the D-Day landing to its pursuit of the retreating German forces.

Inspired by *Saving Private Ryan*, Hanks and Steven Spielberg were among the executive producers of this ambitious television project. Hanks not only directed an episode of the miniseries, but he also wrote another and appeared on camera as a British officer. Tom's son Colin performed as a soldier in the eighth installment of the massive production. The ambitious venture received six Emmy Awards, giving Hanks—in his various technical capacities—several Emmy wins.

On a sad note, in 2002 Tom's first wife, Samantha, was diagnosed with cancer. Even though they had gone through tough times and did not stay in touch regularly, when he

Steven Spielberg and Tom Hanks with Emmy Awards for their World War II miniseries Band of Brothers. *(Landov)*

learned she was sick Tom brought her to Los Angeles to consult with the best medical specialists. However, her condition deteriorated, and she died in March 2002.

New Acting Vistas

Always anxious to further expand his acting range, Tom accepted his first bad-guy screen role in *Road to Perdition* (2002). The violent film is set in the Midwest in 1931. Hanks plays a hit man working for the local gang boss, played by Paul Newman. After Hanks's wife and younger son are murdered, the film follows him and his remaining son as they attempt to escape to safety, but with upsetting consequences.

Road to Perdition met with mixed reviews: Many critics appreciated its technique more than its overall entertainment values. Tom received mixed reviews for his departure from his traditional good-guy role.

In a return to playing characters on the right side of the law, Tom costarred with Leonardo DiCaprio in *Catch Me If You Can* (2002). This film reteamed Hanks with director Steven Spielberg. The DreamWorks production was based on the memoir of Frank Abagnale Jr., who, in 1964 at the age of 16, became a con artist posing in a variety of careers and writing bad checks as he crosses the globe. In the film Tom plays an FBI agent who doggedly pursues the jaunty young criminal, played by DiCaprio.

As the workaholic law enforcer, Hanks provided a solid performance, but some said his stiff character had to compete for audience attention with DiCaprio's chameleon-like performance as the criminal. Made for $52 million, the fast-paced *Catch Me If You Can* grossed $164.4 million in its domestic distribution.

Also in 2002 Tom and his wife Rita invested in the romantic comedy *My Big Fat Greek Wedding*, the screen adaptation of the stage show by Nia Vardalos that was made for the low cost of $5 million. The independent feature proved to be the year's surprise hit, eventually grossing $241 million in domestic distribution.

Looking Ahead

Now in his late forties, Tom Hanks has not slowed down his career pace. As an actor, producer, director, and writer, Tom is respected as a professional and is a favorite of fans around the world. And he is still much in demand in Hollywood. In 2003 preproduction had begun on several new projects with which Tom would be involved. They include *The Polar Express*, a fantasy feature directed by Robert Zemeckis; *The Terminal,* a romantic drama directed by Steven Spielberg; *The Ladykillers*, a remake of a classic British comedy; and *A Cold Case*, a murder mystery.

A few years ago at an awards dinner in his honor, Tom concluded his acceptance speech with the following: "If I'm lucky, I'll have the chance to surprise you [moviegoers] some more." This promise seems likely, considering his constantly crowded filmmaking schedule. Having reached superstar status as the screen's favorite everyman, the somewhat private Hanks seems most comfortable these days portraying a variety of selfless film roles. In choosing screen parts, he says the challenge is "finding things you haven't done before. There's no fun and no future in doing the same thing over again." Above all, he still regards his profession as one that "produces a vast

Rita Wilson and Tom Hanks.
(Landov)

amount of joy. It's hard work if you can get it, but it's great work too."

In recent years Hanks has learned to balance better his hectic career with his home life. He appreciates that "at the end of the day, you have to tell yourself that, 'Well, it's the end of the day.' So, you drive home to your family, have a nice dinner and watch a dart competition on TV. Some actors flog themselves to death. Me, I do not treat my job as if it is a circus act. You do not have to perform around the clock."

Regarding his carefree approach to everyday life, the soft-spoken, modest, and mostly unflappable actor says, "I probably have most of the worries everyone else does, but I just try not to worry too much."

TIME LINE

1956 Tom Hanks born in Concord, California, on July 9, the third of four children

1962 Hanks's parents divorce; Tom and two older siblings (Sandra and Larry) go with their father, while the youngest brother (James) goes with their mother

1974 Graduates from Skyline High School in Oakland, California; matriculates at Chabot Community College in Oakland

1976 Transfers to California State University at Sacramento and enrolls in its theater program

1977 Goes to Cleveland to intern at the Great Lakes Shakespeare Festival; drops out of college to work full time at Sacramento Civic Theater; with actress girlfriend Susan Dillingham (who uses stage name of Samantha Lewes) becomes the parent of son Colin

1978 At the Great Lakes Shakespeare Festival wins Best Actor award from Cleveland Critics Circle; moves to New York City with family

1980 Marries Samantha Lewes; makes feature-film debut in *He Knows You're Alone* (MGM); debuts as costar of ABC-TV sitcom *Bosom Buddies;* family relocates to Los Angeles

1982 Daughter Elizabeth is born; *Bosom Buddies* is canceled; stars in CBS movie *Rona Jaffe's "Mazes and Monsters"*

1984 Enjoys box-office successes with *Splash* (Touchstone) and *Bachelor Party* (Twentieth Century-Fox)

1985 Stars in the films *The Man with One Red Shoe* (Twentieth Century-Fox) and *Volunteers* (TriStar); meets actress Rita Wilson on the Mexico set of *Volunteers*

1986 Leading roles in the movies *The Money Pit* (Universal), *Nothing in Common* (TriStar), and *Every Time We Say Goodbye* (TriStar)

1987 Costars in *Dragnet* (Universal); divorce from Samantha Lewes is finalized

1988 Stars in *Big* (Twentieth Century-Fox) and *Punchline* (Columbia); marries Rita Wilson in Los Angeles on April 30

1989 Headlines *The 'burbs* (Universal) and *Turner & Hooch* (Touchstone); receives Academy Award nomination as Best Actor for *Big*

1990 Stars in *Joe Versus the Volcano* (Warner Bros.) and *The Bonfire of the Vanities* (Warner Bros.); son Chester is born

1992 Plays supporting roles in *Radio Flyer* (Columbia) and *A League of Their Own* (Columbia)

1993 Stars in *Sleepless in Seattle* (TriStar) and *Philadelphia* (TriStar); directs episodes of such TV series as HBO's *Tales from the Crypt*

1994 Plays title role in *Forrest Gump* (Paramount); wins Best Actor Academy Award for *Philadelphia*

1995 Stars in *Apollo 13* (Universal); provides voice-over for *Toy Story* (Disney); is an interviewee in the documentary *The Celluloid Closet;* wins Best Actor Academy Award for *Forrest Gump;* son Truman is born

1996 Writes, directs, acts in, and composes songs for *That Thing You Do!* (Twentieth Century-Fox)

1998 Stars in *Saving Private Ryan* (Paramount/DreamWorks) and *You've Got Mail* (Warner Bros.); executive produces the HBO miniseries *From the Earth to the Moon*

1999 Repeats voice of Sheriff Woody for *Toy Story 2* (Disney); stars in *The Green Mile* (Warner Bros.); is nominated for a Best Actor Oscar for *Saving Private Ryan*; wins an Emmy Award for Outstanding Miniseries (*From the Earth to the Moon*); is honored by the American Museum of the Moving Image

2000 Stars in and produces *Cast Away* (Twentieth Century-Fox/DreamWorks)

2001 Produces the HBO miniseries *Band of Brothers*

2002 Headlines *Road to Perdition* (DreamWorks/Twentieth Century-Fox) and *Catch Me If You Can* (DreamWorks); with Rita Wilson produces the feature film *My Big Fat Greek Wedding* (IFC); winner of several Emmy Awards for *Band of Brothers*; is honored with Lifetime Achievement award by the American Film Institute

2003 Begins preproduction of the movies *The Polar Express, Terminal, The Ladykillers,* and *A Cold Case*

HOW TO BECOME AN ACTOR

THE JOB

The imitation or basic development of a character for presentation to an audience may seem like a glamorous and fairly easy job. In reality, it is demanding, tiring work that requires a special talent.

An actor must first find an available part in some upcoming production. This may be in a comedy, drama, musical, or opera. Then, having read and studied the part, the actor must audition before the director and other people who have control of the production. This requirement is often waived for established artists. In film and television, actors must also complete screen tests, which are scenes recorded on film, at times performed with other actors, which are later viewed by the director and producer of the film.

If selected for the part, the actor must spend hundreds of hours in rehearsal and must memorize many lines and cues. This is especially true in live theater; in film and television actors may spend less time in rehearsal and sometimes improvise their lines before the camera, often performing several attempts, or "takes," before the director is satisfied. Television actors often take advantage of TelePrompTers, which scroll lines on a screen in front of performing actors. Radio actors generally read from a script, and therefore their rehearsal times are usually shorter.

In addition to such mechanical duties, the actor must determine the essence of the character he or she is auditioning for, and the relation of that character to the overall scheme of the production. Radio actors must be especially skilled in expressing character and emotion through voice alone. In many film and theater roles actors must also sing and dance and spend additional time rehearsing songs and perfecting choreography. Certain roles require actors to perform various stunts, some of which can be quite dangerous. Specially trained performers usually complete these stunts. Others work as stand-ins or body doubles. These actors are chosen for specific features and appear on film in place of the lead actor; this is often the case in films requiring nude or seminude scenes. Many television programs, such as game shows, also feature models, who generally assist the host of the program.

Actors in the theater may perform the same part many times a week for weeks, months, and sometimes years. This allows them to develop the role, but it can also become tedious. Actors in films may spend several weeks involved in a production, which often takes place on location (that is, in different parts of the world). Television actors involved in a series, such as a soap opera or a situation comedy, also may play the same role for years, generally in 13-week cycles. For these actors, however, their lines change from week to week and even from day to day, and much time is spent rehearsing their new lines.

While studying and perfecting their craft, many actors work as extras, the nonspeaking characters who appear in the background on screen or stage. Many actors also continue training throughout their careers. A great deal of an actor's time is spent attending auditions.

REQUIREMENTS

High School

There are no minimum educational requirements to become an actor. However, at least a high school diploma is recommended. In high school English classes you will learn about the history of drama and the development of strong characters. Take music classes to help you develop your voice and ability to read music, which are valuable skills for any actor, even those who do not perform many musical roles.

Postsecondary Training

As acting becomes more and more involved with the various facets of society, a college degree will become more important to those who hope to have an acting career. An actor who has completed a liberal arts program is thought to be more capable of understanding the wide variety of roles that are available. Therefore, it is strongly recommended that aspiring actors complete at least a bachelor's degree program in theater or the dramatic arts. In addition, graduate degrees in the fine arts or in drama are nearly always required should the individual decide to teach dramatic arts.

College can also provide acting experience for the hopeful actor. More than 500 colleges and universities throughout the country offer dramatic arts programs and present theatrical performances. Actors and directors recommend that those interested in acting gain as much experience as possible through acting in high school and college plays or in those offered by community groups. Training beyond college is recommended, especially for actors interested in entering the theater. Joining acting workshops, such as the Actors Studio, can often be highly competitive.

Other Requirements

Prospective actors will be required not only to have a great talent for acting but also a great determination to succeed in the theater and motion pictures. They must be able to memorize hundreds of lines and should have a good speaking voice. The ability to sing and dance is important for increasing the opportunities for the young actor. Almost all actors are required to audition for a part before they receive the role. In film and television actors will generally complete screen tests to see how they appear on film. In all fields of acting, a love of performing is a must. It might take many years for an actor to achieve any success, if they achieve it at all.

Performers on Broadway stages must be members of the Actors' Equity Association before being cast. While union membership may not always be required, many actors find it advantageous to belong to a union that covers their particular field of performing arts. These organizations include the Actors' Equity Association (stage), Screen Actors Guild or Screen Extras Guild (motion pictures and television films), or American Federation of Television and Radio Artists (TV, recording, and radio). In addition, some actors may benefit from membership in the American Guild of Variety Artists (nightclubs and so on), American Guild of Musical Artists (opera and ballet), or organizations such as the Hebrew Actors Union or Italian Actors Union for productions in those languages.

EXPLORING

The best way to explore this career is to participate in school or local theater productions. Even working on the props or lighting crew will provide insight into the field.

Also, attend as many dramatic productions as possible and try to talk with people who either are currently in the theater or have been at one time. They can offer advice to individuals interested in a career in the theater.

There are many books about acting that concern not only how to perform, but also the nature of the work, its offerings, advantages, and disadvantages.

EMPLOYERS

Motion pictures, television, and the stage are the largest fields of employment for actors, with television commercials representing as much as 60 percent of all acting jobs. Most of the opportunities for employment in these fields are either in Los Angeles or in New York. On the stage, even the road shows often have their beginning in New York, with the selection of actors conducted there along with rehearsals. However, nearly every city and most communities present local and regional theater productions.

As cable television networks continue to produce more and more of their own programs and films, they will become a major provider of employment for actors. Home video will also continue to create new acting jobs, as will the music video business.

The lowest numbers of actors are employed for stage work. In addition to Broadway shows and regional theater, there are employment opportunities for stage actors in summer stock, at resorts, and on cruise ships.

STARTING OUT

Probably the best way to enter acting is to start with high school, local, or college productions and to gain as much experience as possible on that level. Very rarely is an inexperienced actor given an opportunity to perform onstage or in a film in New York or Hollywood. The field is extremely difficult to enter; the more experience and ability beginners have, however, the greater the possibilities for entrance.

Those venturing to New York or Hollywood are encouraged first to have enough money to support themselves during the long waiting and searching period normally required before a job is found. Most will list themselves with a casting agency that will help them find a part as an extra or a bit player, either in theater or film. These agencies keep names on file along with photographs and a description of the individual's features and experience, and if a part comes along that may be suitable, they contact that person. Very often, however, names are added to their lists only when the number of people in a particular physical category is low. For instance, the agency may not have enough athletic young women on its roster, and if the applicant happens to fit this description, her name is added.

ADVANCEMENT

New actors will normally start with bit parts and will have only a few lines to speak, if any. The normal progression would then be landing larger supporting roles and then, in the case of theater, possibly a role as an understudy for one of the main actors. The understudy usually has an opportunity to fill in should the main actor be unable to give a performance. Many film and television actors get their start in commercials or by appearing in government and commercially sponsored public service announcements, films, and programs. Other actors join the afternoon soap operas and continue on to evening programs. Many actors also have started in on-camera roles such as presenting the weather segment of a local news program. Once an actor has gained experience, he or she may go on to play stronger supporting roles or even leading roles in stage, television, or film productions. From there, an actor may go on to stardom. Only a very small number of actors ever reach that pinnacle, however.

Some actors eventually go into other, related occupations and become drama coaches, drama teachers, producers, stage directors, motion picture directors, television directors, radio directors, stage managers, casting directors, or artist and repertoire managers. Others may combine one or more of these functions while continuing their careers.

EARNINGS

The wage scale for actors is largely controlled through bargaining agreements reached by various unions in negotiations with producers. These agreements normally control the minimum salaries, hours of work permitted per week, and other conditions of employment. In addition, each artist enters into a separate contract that may provide for higher salaries.

In 2002 the minimum daily salary of any member of the Screen Actors Guild (SAG) in a speaking role was $655, or $2,272 for a five-day workweek. Motion picture actors may also receive additional payments known as residuals as part of their guaranteed salary. Many motion picture actors receive residuals whenever films, TV shows, and TV commercials in which they appear are rerun, sold for TV exhibition, or put on DVD. Residuals often exceed the actor's original salary and account for about one-third of all actors' income.

A wide range of earnings can be seen when reviewing the Actors' Equity Association's *Annual Report 2000,* which includes a breakdown of average weekly salaries by contract type and location. According to the report, for example, those in off-Broadway productions earned an average weekly salary of $642 during the 1999–2000 season. Other average weekly earnings for the same period include: San Francisco Bay Area theater, $329; New

England area theater, $236; Walt Disney World in Orlando, Florida, $704; and Chicago area theater, $406. The report concludes that the median weekly salary for all contract areas is $457. Most actors do not work 52 weeks per year; in fact, the report notes that of the 38,013 members in good standing only 16,976 were employed. The majority of those employed, approximately 12,000, had annual earnings ranging from $1 to $15,000.

According to the U.S. Department of Labor, the median yearly earning of all actors was $25,920 in 2000. The department also reported the lowest paid 10 percent earned less than $12,700 annually, while the highest paid 10 percent made more than $93,620.

The annual earnings of persons in television and movies are affected by frequent periods of unemployment. According to SAG, most of its members earn less than $7,500 a year from acting jobs. Unions offer health, welfare, and pension funds for members working more than a set number of weeks a year. Some actors are eligible for paid vacation and sick time, depending on the work contract.

In all fields, well-known actors have salary rates above the minimums, and the salaries of the few top stars are many times higher. Actors in television series may earn tens of thousands of dollars per week, while a few may earn as much as $1 million or more per week. Salaries for these actors vary considerably and are negotiated individually. In film, top stars may earn as much as $20 million per film, and, after receiving a percentage of the gross earned by the film, these stars can earn far, far more.

Until recent years, female film stars tended to earn lower salaries than their male counterparts; stars such as Julia Roberts, Jodie Foster, Halle Berry, and others has started to reverse that trend. The average annual earnings for all motion picture actors, however, are usually low for all but the best-known performers because of the periods of unemployment.

WORK ENVIRONMENT

Actors work under varying conditions. Those employed in motion pictures may work in air-conditioned studios one week and be on location in a hot desert the next.

Those in stage productions perform under all types of conditions. The number of hours employed per day or week varies, as does the number of weeks employed per year. Stage actors normally perform eight shows per week with any additional performances paid for as overtime. The basic workweek after the show opens is about 36 hours unless major changes in the play are needed. The number of hours worked per week is considerably more before the opening because of rehearsals. Evening work is a natural part of a stage actor's life. Rehearsals often are held at night and over holidays and weekends. If the play goes on the road, much traveling will be involved.

A number of actors cannot receive unemployment compensation when they are waiting for their next part, primarily because they have not worked enough to meet the minimum eligibility requirements for compensation. Sick leaves and paid vacations are not usually available to the actor. However, union actors who earn the minimum qualifications now receive full medical and health insurance under all the actors' unions. Those who earn health-plan benefits for 10 years become eligible for a pension upon retirement. The acting field is very uncertain. Aspirants never know whether they will be able to get into the profession, and, once in, there are uncertainties as to whether the show will be well-received and, if not, whether the actors' talent can survive a bad show.

OUTLOOK

Employment in acting is expected to grow faster than the average through 2010, according to the U.S. Department of Labor. There are a number of reasons for this. The growth of satellite and cable television in the past decade has created a demand for more actors, especially as the cable networks produce more and more of their own programs and films. The rise of home video and DVD has also created new acting jobs, as more and more films are made strictly for the home-video market. Many resorts built in the 1980s and 1990s present their own theatrical productions, providing more job opportunities for actors. Jobs in theater, however, face pressure as the cost of mounting a production rises and as many nonprofit and smaller theaters lose their funding.

Despite the growth in opportunities, there are many more actors than there are roles, and this is likely to remain true for years to come. This is true in all areas of the arts, including radio, television, motion pictures, and theater, and even those who are employed are normally employed during only a small portion of the year. Many actors must supplement their income by working at other jobs, such as secretaries, waiters, or taxi drivers, for example. Almost all performers are members of more than one union in order to take advantage of various opportunities as they become available.

It should be recognized that of the 105,000 or so actors in the United States today, an average of only about 16,000 are employed at any one time. Of these, few are able to support themselves on their earnings from acting, and fewer still will ever achieve stardom. Most actors work for many years before becoming known, and most of these do not rise above supporting roles. The vast majority of actors, meanwhile, are still looking for the right break. There are many more applicants in all areas than there are positions. As with most careers in the arts, people enter this career out of a genuine love of acting.

TO LEARN MORE ABOUT ACTORS

BOOKS

Bruder, Melissa. *A Practical Handbook for the Actor.* New York: Vintage, 1986.

Lee, Robert L. *Everything about Theater!: The Guidebook of Theater Fundamentals.* Colorado Springs, Colo.: Meriwether, 1996.

Quinlan, Kathryn A. *Actor.* Mankato, Minn.: Capstone Press, 1998.

Stevens, Chambers. *Magnificent Monologues for Kids.* South Pasadena, Calif.: Sandcastle, 1999.

ORGANIZATIONS

The Actors' Equity Association is a professional union for actors in theater and "live" industrial productions, stage managers, some directors, and choreographers.

Actors' Equity Association

165 West 46th Street

New York, NY 10036

Tel: 212-869-8530

E-mail: info@actorsequity.org

http://www.actorsequity.org

This union represents television and radio performers, including actors, announcers, dancers, disc jockeys, newspersons, singers, specialty acts, sportscasters, and stuntpersons.

American Federation of Television and Radio
 Artists

260 Madison Avenue

New York, NY 10016-2402

Tel: 212-532-0800

E-mail: aftra@aftra.com

http://www.aftra.com

A directory of theatrical programs may be purchased from NAST. For answers to a number of frequently asked questions concerning education, visit the NAST website.

National Association of Schools of Theater (NAST)

11250 Roger Bacon Drive, Suite 21

Reston, VA 20190

Tel: 703-437-0700

E-mail: info@arts-accredit.org

http://www.arts-accredit.org/nast

The Screen Actors Guild (SAG) provides general information on actors, directors, and producers. Visit the SAG website for more information.

Screen Actors Guild (SAG)

5757 Wilshire Boulevard

Los Angeles, CA 90036-3600

Tel: 323-954-1600

http://www.sag.com

For information about opportunities in not-for-profit theaters, contact

Theatre Communications Group

355 Lexington Avenue

New York, NY 10017

Tel: 212-697-5230

E-mail: tcg@tcg.org

http://www.tcg.org

This site has information for beginners on acting and the acting business.

Acting Workshop On-Line

http://www.redbirdstudio.com/AWOL/acting2.html

HOW TO BECOME A PRODUCER

THE JOB

The primary role of a producer is to organize and secure the financial backing necessary to undertake a motion picture project. The director, by contrast, creates the film from the screenplay. Despite this general distinction, the producer often takes part in creative decisions, and occasionally one person is both the producer and director. On some small projects, such as a nature or historical documentary for a public-television broadcast, the producer might also be the writer and camera operator.

The job of a producer generally begins in the preproduction stage of filmmaking with the selection of a movie idea from a script or other material. Some films are made from original screenplays, while others are adapted from books. If a book is selected, the producer must first purchase the rights from the author or his or her publishing company, and a writer must be hired to adapt the book into a screenplay format. Producers are usually inundated with scripts from writers and others who have ideas for a movie. Producers may have their own ideas for a motion picture and will hire a writer to write the screenplay. Occasionally a studio will approach a producer, typically a producer who has had many commercially or artistically successful films in the past, with a project.

After selecting a project, the producer will find a director, the technical staff, and the star actor or actors to participate in the film. Along with the script and screenwriter, these essential people are referred to as the package. Packaging is sometimes arranged with the help of talent agencies. It is the package that the producer tries to sell to an investor to obtain the necessary funds to finance the salaries and cost of the film.

There are three common sources for financing a film: major studios, production companies, and individual investors. A small number of producers have enough money to pay for their own projects. Major studios are the largest source of money, and they finance most of the big-budget films. Although some studios have full-time producers on staff, they hire self-employed, or *independent producers*, for many projects. Large production companies often have the capital resources to fund projects that they feel will be commercially successful. On the smaller end of the scale, producers of documentary films commonly approach individual donors; foundations; art agencies of federal, state, and local governments; and even family members and churches. The National Endowment for the Humanities and the National Endowment for the Arts are major federal benefactors of cinema.

Raising money from individual investors can occupy much of the producer's time. Fund-raising may be done on the telephone, as well as in conferences, business lunches, and even at parties. The producer may also look for a distributor for the film even before the production begins.

Obtaining the necessary financing does not guarantee a film will be made. After raising the money, the producer takes the basic plan of the package and tries to work it into a developed project. The script may be rewritten several times, the full cast of actors is hired, salaries are negotiated, and logistical problems, such as the location of the filming, are worked out. On some projects it might be the director who handles these tasks, or the director may work with the producer. Most major film projects do not get beyond this complicated stage of development.

During the production phase, the producer tries to keep the project on schedule and the spending within the established budget. Other production tasks include the review of dailies, which are prints of the day's filming. As the head of the project, the producer is ultimately responsible for resolving all problems, including conflicts such as those between the director and an actor, and the director and the studio. If the film is successfully completed, the producer monitors its distribution and may participate in the publicity and advertising of the film.

To accomplish the many and varied tasks the position requires, producers hire a number of subordinates, such as associate producers, sometimes called coproducers, line producers, and production assistants. Job titles, however, vary from project to project. In general, *associate producers* work directly under the producer and oversee the major areas of the project, such as the budget. *Line producers* handle the day-to-day operations of the project. *Production assistants* may perform substantive tasks, such as reviewing scripts, but others are hired to run errands. Another title, *executive producer*, often refers to the person who puts up the money, such as a studio executive, but it is sometimes an honorary title with no functional relevance to the project.

REQUIREMENTS

There is no minimum educational requirement for becoming a producer. Many producers, however, are college graduates, and many also have a business degree or other previous business experience. They must not only be talented salespeople and administrators but also have a thorough understanding of films and motion picture technology. Such understanding, of course, only comes from experience.

High School

High school courses that will be of assistance to future producers include speech, mathematics, business, psychology, and English.

Postsecondary Training

Formal study of film, television, communications, theater, writing, English literature, or art is helpful, as the producer must have the background to know whether an idea or script is worth pursuing. Many entry-level positions in the film industry are given to people who have studied liberal arts, cinema, or both.

In the United States there are more than 1,000 colleges, universities, and trade schools that offer classes in film or television studies; more than 120 of these offer undergraduate programs, and more than 50 grant master's degrees. A small number of Ph.D. programs also exist.

Graduation from a film or television course of study does not guarantee employment in the industry. Some programs are quite expensive, costing more than $50,000 in tuition alone for three years of study. Others do not have the resources to allow all students to make their own films.

Programs in Los Angeles and New York City, the major centers of the entertainment industry, may provide the best opportunities for making contacts that can be of benefit when seeking employment.

Other Requirements

Producers come from a wide variety of backgrounds. Some start out as magazine editors, business school graduates, actors, or secretaries, messengers, and production assistants for a film studio. Many have never formally studied film.

Most producers, however, get their position through several years of experience in the industry, perseverance, and a keen sense for what projects will be artistically and commercially successful.

EXPLORING

There are many ways to gain experience in filmmaking. Some high schools have film and video clubs, for example, or courses on the use of motion picture equipment. Experience in high school or college theater can also be useful. One of the best ways to gain experience is to volunteer for a student or low-budget film project; positions on such projects are often advertised in local trade publications. Community cable stations also hire volunteers and may even offer internships.

EMPLOYERS

Many producers in the field are self-employed. Others are salaried employees of film companies, television networks, and television stations. The greatest concentration of motion picture producers is in Hollywood and New York City. Hollywood alone has more than 2,000 producers.

STARTING OUT

Becoming a producer is similar to becoming president of a company. Unless a person is independently wealthy and can finance whichever projects he or she chooses, prior experience in the field is necessary. Because there are so few positions, even with experience it is extremely difficult to become a successful producer.

Most motion picture producers have attained their position only after years of moving up the industry ladder. Thus, it is important to concentrate on immediate goals, such as getting an entry-level position in a film company. Some enter the field by getting a job as a production assistant. An entry-level production assistant may photocopy scripts for actors to use, assist in setting up equipment, or perform other menial tasks, often for very little or even no pay. While a production assistant's work is often tedious and of little seeming reward, it nevertheless does expose one to the intricacies of filmmaking and, more important, creates an opportunity to make contacts with others in the industry.

Those interested in the field should approach film companies, television stations, or the television networks about employment opportunities as a production assistant. Small television stations often provide the best opportunity for those who are interested in television producing. Positions may also be listed in trade publications.

ADVANCEMENT

There is little room for advancement because producers are at the top of their profession. Advancement for producers is generally measured by the types of projects they do, increased earnings, and respect in the field. At television stations, a producer can advance to program director. Some producers become directors or make enough money to finance their own projects.

EARNINGS

Producers are generally paid a percentage of the project's profits or a fee negotiated between the producer and a studio. The U.S. Department of Labor (USDL) reports that producers and directors earned average salaries of $41,030 in 2000. Salaries ranged from less than $21,050 to more than $87,770. Producers of highly successful films can earn $200,000 or more, while those who make low-budget or documentary films might earn considerably less than the average. In general, producers in the film industry earn more than television producers. The USDL reports that producers employed in the motion picture industry had average earnings of $50,280 in 2000, while those employed in television broadcasting averaged $34,630. Entry-level production assistants can earn from less than minimum wage to $15,000 per year.

WORK ENVIRONMENT

Producers have greater control over their working conditions than most other people working in the motion picture industry. They may have the autonomy of choosing their own projects, setting their own hours, and delegating duties to others as necessary. The work often brings considerable personal satisfaction. But it is not without constraints. Producers must work within a stressful schedule complicated by competing work pressures and often-daily crises. Each project brings a significant financial and professional risk. Long hours and weekend work are common. Most producers must provide for their own health insurance and other benefits.

OUTLOOK

Employment for producers is expected to grow faster than the average through 2010, according to the U.S. Department of Labor. Though opportunities may increase with the expansion of cable and satellite television, news programs, DVD rentals, and an increased overseas demand for American-made films, competition for jobs will be high. Live theater and entertainment will also provide job openings. Some positions will be available as current producers leave the workforce.

TO LEARN MORE ABOUT PRODUCERS

BOOKS

Erikson, Gunnar, Mark Halloran, and Harris Tulchin. *The Independent Film Producer's Survival Guide: A Business and Legal Sourcebook.* Omnibus Press, 2002.

Harmon, Renee. *The Beginning Filmmaker's Business Guide: Financial, Legal, Marketing, and Distribution Basics of Making Movies.* New York: Walker & Company, 1993.

Houghton, Buck. *What a Producer Does: The Art of Moviemaking (Not the Business).* Los Angeles: Silman-James Press, 1991.

Levy, Frederick. *Hollywood 101: The Film Industry.* Renaissance Books, 2000.

Rensin, David. *The Mailroom: Hollywood History from the Bottom Up.* New York: Random House, 2003.

ORGANIZATIONS

Visit the PGA website to read an on-line version of *Point of View* magazine, which focuses on the role of producers in the motion picture and television industries.

Producers Guild of America (PGA)

8530 Wilshire Boulevard, Suite 450

Beverly Hills, CA 90211

http://www.producersguild.org

The Broadcast Education Association is a good source of information on scholarships and grants, interest divisions, and filmmaking publications.

Broadcast Education Association

1771 N Street, NW

Washington, DC 20036-2891

http://www.beaweb.org

TO LEARN MORE ABOUT TOM HANKS

BOOKS

Brode, Douglas. *The Films of Steven Spielberg*. New York: Kensington Citadel, 2000.

Gardner, David. *Tom Hanks*. London: Blake, 1999.

Kramer, Barbara. *Tom Hanks: Superstar*. Berkeley Heights, N.J.: Enslow, 2001.*

Lee, Linda. *Tom Hanks*. New York: People Profiles/Time, 1999.

McAvoy, Jim. *Tom Hanks*. Philadelphia: Chelsea House, 1999.*

Parish, James Robert, and Don E. Stanke. *Hollywood Baby Boomers*. New York: Garland, 1992.

Pfeiffer, Lee and Michael Lewis. *The Films of Tom Hanks*. Secaucus, N.J.: Citadel/Carol, 1996.

Quinlan, David. *Tom Hanks: A Career in Orbit*. London: Batsford, 1997.

Trakin, Roy. *Tom Hanks: Journey to Stardom* (updated ed.). New York: St. Martin's, 1995.

Wallner, Rosemary. *Tom Hanks: Academy Award-Winning Actor*. Edina, Minn: Abdo & Daughters, 1994.*

Wheeler, Jill C. *Tom Hanks*. Edina, Minn.: Abdo & Daughters, 2002.*

* Young Adult book

WEBSITES

Internet Movie Database

http://www.imdb.com

Tom Hanks Appreciation Society

http://www.tomhanksweb.com/home.html

Tom Hanks Land

http://www.tomhanksland.com

Tom Hanks Online

http://www.geocities.com/tomhanks00

INDEX

ABOUT THE AUTHOR

James Robert Parish, a former entertainment reporter, publicist, and book series editor, is the author of numerous biographies and reference books on the entertainment industry, including *Steven Spielberg: Filmmaker, Whitney Houston, Gus Van Sant, The Hollywood Book of Love, The Hollywood Book of Death, Jason Biggs, Whoopi Goldberg, Rosie O'Donnell's Story, The Unofficial "Murder, She Wrote" Casebook, Let's Talk—America's Favorite TV Talk Show Hosts, The Great Cop Pictures, Ghosts and Angels in Hollywood Films, Prison Pictures from Hollywood, Hollywood's Great Love Teams*, and *The RKO Gals*. Most recently he wrote the critically lauded *Encyclopedia of Ethnic Groups in Hollywood*. Mr. Parish is a frequent on-camera commentator on cable and network television for documentaries about the performing arts. Mr. Parish resides in Studio City, California.